How To Start And Run A Small Book Publishing Company

By Peter I. Hupalo

Library of Congress Control Number: 2002106122
ISBN 0-9671624-3-2

Printed in the United States of America

HCM Publishing
P.O. Box 18093
West Saint Paul, MN 55118

Dedication

This book is dedicated to Patricia J. Bell, author of *The Prepublishing Handbook: What You Should Know Before You Publish Your First Book*. Pat first introduced me to the world of independent publishing through her classes at Open U. In addition to being a great instructor, Pat is a champion of independent publishing in Minnesota.

****

Other Books By Peter Hupalo:

Thinking Like An Entrepreneur: How To Make Intelligent Business Decisions That Will Lead To Success In Building And Growing Your Own Company

Becoming An Investor: Building Wealth By Investing In Stocks, Bonds, And Mutual Funds

Table Of Contents

So, You Want To Self-Publish Your Own Book?

I published my first book, *Thinking Like An Entrepreneur: How To Make Intelligent Business Decisions That Will Lead To Success In Building And Growing Your Own Company*, back in 1999. I've always enjoyed business and writing, so I figured self-publishing a book would be fun.

Promptly after starting HCM Publishing, I was fortunate to subscribe to some online publisher lists, which were useful to me in learning about publishing. One of those lists is now defunct. The other list, Publish-L, is still around. You can learn more about the list and subscribe to it by visiting Publish-L.com.

Many publishers have helped me along the way, so I've made it a point to help other new publishers. I've answered hundreds, if not thousands, of publisher questions on Publish-L. And, the list has many other experienced publishers who are eager to help new publishers and authors.

Because no book can answer every specific question you have about publishing, I highly recommend anyone who starts a publishing company subscribe to an online small publisher list, such as Publish-L. Another popular list is Pub-Forum (www.pub-forum.net), which also has many knowledgeable and experienced publishers.

With any list, feel free to be a 'lurker' until you decide you're comfortable with a list. A 'lurker' is someone who reads the messages, but doesn't post. Online, there's nothing sinister in being a 'lurker.'

I also recommend subscribing to a publishing list to learn about the *current* quality of service providers, such as fulfillment companies, cover designers, book printers, etc., in the publishing industry.

For example, what book printers do experienced publishers recommend? By knowing other publishers, you'll get valuable insight into which companies are easy to work with and which companies should be avoided. Suppose you're thinking of printing your book with Iggy Wiggy Wack Printing (a name I just made up). Is Iggy Wiggy Wack a good printer? Or, do they stink?

Your search for book printers, cover designers, PR experts, and many other useful service providers can begin online at a publisher discussion list. Find out who experienced publishers recommend. *As a new publisher, I'd recommend working with only the more established, quality service providers because you're just learning and you won't know what questions to ask to distinguish quality providers from second rate (or worse!) sources.*

For example, maybe Iggy Wiggy Wack's prices are great. But, is their hardcover price only for glued hardcover or for smythe sewn hardcover? Suppose Iggy Wiggy Wack is confused by the question and answers your question with a question, "Sewn. You mean like with a needle and thread?"

That's a good indication that Iggy Wiggy Wack might not be the printer for you!

The problem is that when you're just starting, you might not know enough to distinguish between a smythe sewn hardcover and a glued hardcover. You might not know what questions to ask to determine if the service provider really understands what he's doing or if he's trying to fleece you. You won't know what's price competitive and what isn't. You might wind up comparing apples to oranges and buying a less expensive orange when you wanted an apple. As you gain experience, you'll develop a sixth sense for avoiding bad service providers by what they claim and how they claim it.

As the old saying goes, "To avoid making mistakes, you need experience, and experience comes from making mistakes." But, when you're just starting your company, mistakes can kill your company or your enthusiasm.

I recall Steve Jobs discussing Pixar, his animated film production company. For *Toy Story*, he negotiated a deal with Disney that many investors thought wasn't acceptably profitable and gave everything away to Disney. They missed the key point. Jobs' goal was to learn about the animated film industry and partnering and working with Disney gave Pixar an experience most other companies interested in film animation and distribution lacked. Pixar's profitability would come from the titles it produced after *Toy Story*, when it had gained experience and insight from Disney.

When I first printed *Thinking Like An Entrepreneur*, I chose the printing company I felt had the best overall reputation among experienced publishers (Thomson-Shore, Inc.). They not only did a great job, but they helped me understand a great deal about the process of book production. Even though their quote was a bit higher than their competitors, I knew there was value in working with a highly-respected printer who had a reputation for being easy to work with.

Once you've been though the process a time or two and have some experience, then you might try to save a few bucks by working with Iggy Wiggy Wack!

How To Start And Run A Small Book Publishing Company can potentially save readers thousands of dollars in mistakes. For example, overprinting a first book, rather than looking at the first press run as a test, is a common mistake made by new publishers, who needlessly tie up thousands of dollars in inventory. A reprint also offers a chance to add valuable testimonials to the book.

How To Start And Run A Small Book Publishing Company can also save you countless hours in understanding things such as postscript and PMS colors. And, I hope it will offer some business insight that could lead to great success for your new publishing company. Learning a bit in advance can be the difference between starting a financially successful publishing company and becoming disillusioned with self-publishing.

In addition to helping new publishers, I believe this book will be valuable reading for experienced publishers looking for business insight into marketing, selecting authors, order fulfillment, and the many other aspects of book publishing. Experienced publishers will learn about inventory accounting, the tax deductibility of complimentary copies, book pricing, sales tax issues, copyright valuation, and many other more advanced topics that often aren't adequately addressed in other self-publishing books.

So, you want to write and self-publish a book? I don't know what your personal motivations are for wanting to self-publish. Usually, a person who wants to write and publish a book wishes to make some money, share experience and help people, or promote a cause. Whatever your reason for wanting to begin a small publishing company, this book will help you learn what you need to know.

If your goal is financial, publishing is a great industry. Profit margins and inventory turnover can be very high, and many people have become wealthy by starting and running publishing companies. The key to success rests in effectively marketing your company's books. That's why the biggest chapter of this book is devoted to marketing. Master book marketing, and you'll be successful!

Fiction Versus Non-Fiction

Writing fiction for money is much like trying to become an actor or an athlete. There are many, many people who *want* to do it. Many people who actually *try* to do it. And, most people *don't* succeed. It's a numbers problem.

There are two possibilities. One, become a bestselling author. If you do, you'll make oodles of money. You'll beat the odds. Two, sell a sequence of books, such as the *Nancy Drew* stories. If you build a readership, you can do well.

I'm not going to tell you it's easy to become successful selling fiction. Many self-publishing books tell the story of three or four carefully chosen fiction authors who have become immensely successful with self-published fiction. But those books don't show the thousands of examples of fiction failure! If your dream is to self-publish fiction, I'd say, "Go for it." But know that it'll probably be a tough road.

Quite a while ago, I saw a film called *Rudy*. The film was about a short fellow who really wanted to play football at Notre Dame. His goal was to get into a game and play, despite the other players all being bigger and better suited to playing football. Rudy worked *harder* than anybody else. He made the team. He continued to work harder than anybody else and, eventually, he realized his goal of getting into a game for a few minutes.

Many people said the film was about the triumph of will and determination and that Rudy was a paragon of success in following a dream. I say the film is a good example of a poor fellow misled into following a bad choice. *Talent* is a key to success. In a game like football, size matters! Anyone who tries to deny that fact is setting himself up for failure. The same is true in trying to publish fiction or achieve anything else in life.

Success in life is a function of *desire and talent and conditions*. If any of those are too seriously stacked against you, consider finding a better endeavor! Find out how to use your natural talents, rather than pursing what society has conditioned you to believe is important.

Rudy could have spent his time achieving something he had a natural talent to do. He could have spent that time becoming a doctor. Or a gymnast. Or a successful and rich entrepreneur. He could have written and self-published a book! Hard work into any of those endeavors would probably have led to more lasting success than a few minutes of 'on field' time.

Consider the opportunity cost of pursuing something that is likely to fail. But, if you do achieve something silly, try to get a film made about it or sell subsidiary rights! Sell endorsements! Rudy, a fellow with no talent for football, got on the football field for only a few seconds, had absolutely no impact on the game's outcome, and had a movie made about it! How many *talented* college football players are able to leverage that much success from their glory days in football?

One key to success in self-publishing is leveraging your success to achieve more success.

Every self-publishing expert seems to agree that non-fiction offers better opportunities for authors and self-publishers. In any case, if you write to write, write what you want. I do. There's nothing wrong with this. If you want more sales, write to the market. No matter what you write or publish, *learn* about the business of publishing.

I recommend focusing upon related books that can be cross promoted. Don't focus upon books which will have a limited shelf life. *Build your backlist.* Understand your market and be entrepreneurial in reaching your market.

Also, consider other options for your books: Translations, adaptations into film, selling subsidiary rights, serialization, etc. This adds to your company's profitability. For example, selling excerpts of your book in places such as *Parade* with its 81 million subscribers not only yields thousands of dollars for the excerpt, but leads to more book sales. As Pauli tells *Rocky*, you need to know how to get "media exposure."

Let's work backwards. Assume you hope to make $1 million with books. Why not? Everyone likes that number! It will probably take more than a couple of years, so due to living expenses and taxes, you'll probably need to earn at least twice that amount or $2 million.

Suppose you have upper-mid-priced books and you can earn $4 per copy profit after all expenses. You need to sell 500,000 books! That's a lot of books! Figure that, even with good marketing, you'd be very happy to sell 20,000 copies of each of your titles on average. That means you need to publish about 25 books in our estimates. Now, as an author, I know I don't have 25 books inside of me. Not 25 good ones anyway!

The solution is to publish other author's books if money is your goal. You'll make less per book, but your ability to feed more books into your pipeline should more than offset that. Overall, publishing has been very profitable as an industry. Even though publishers make little per book, publishing is a potential gold mine.

If you don't want to publish others, but want to make more money, you could stay "me-focused," as many authors do. Stephen Covey comes to mind. He has about a hundred "Seven Habits" products in addition to his bestselling books.

Many bestselling authors generate tremendous profits from just their identity and celebrity status. For example, in addition to book sales, many bestselling authors charge $10,000 or more to give a speech. A speech or two a month really add up to serious money!

On the other hand, it's OK if you don't want to speak publicly. I grew up in the Midwest, where we have a saying, "Fools' names and fools' faces often appear in public places." Many people have an inherent aversion to self-promotion.

A big advantage to self-publishing (or running your own business as an entrepreneur) is that you get to choose exactly what you do with your life. Run your business the way *you* want. Promote your books the way *you* want.

Many successful authors use books as promotional tools to promote other products or services. For example, many investment gurus write books to market their $200 investment newsletters or seminars. Books can serve as promotion for other products, if that's your goal. If not, that's OK too. But, if you want to remain an "industry of one," becoming a celebrity or "Martha Stewarting" yourself is highly profitable.

Ultimately, writing and publishing should fit in with your other life goals and your self-perception. Do what you want, and you'll probably be successful! Force yourself to do something you don't really enjoy, and success becomes more difficult. Do what you want, and it won't even feel like work.

Getting Things Done. Of Flow And Thrashing

I have a theory about getting things done. In computer systems, sometimes, if you get too many different things happening, so much time is spent transferring the computer's attention from one thing to another and back that no computer microchip processor time is left to actually *do* any of the computing. So, nothing gets done. The system thrashes back and forth between too many projects.

I think the same is true of people. We want to do *too much*. So, we undertake one more project, meaning that a project initially started doesn't get finished and so becomes useless. I think focus is the key to success. Try to throw yourself into one project completely and do nothing else until it's finished.

Some might argue that this leads to becoming too narrow. I don't think so. To finish any project is going to take a certain number of hours. Whether those hours are spent all together or spread out over years doesn't matter. So, rather than spending an hour a day for a year, spend several hours a day for a few months. Then, go do whatever you want to do the other months, so you remain a well-rounded person.

If possible, become completely absorbed in what you're doing. Get in the flow of it, as recommended in *Flow: The Psychology of Optimal*

Experience by Mihaly Csikszentmihalyi. The author also has another book called *Creativity*. Both give insight into being productive and creative. I find when I do a lot with one project each day, I'm more motivated to get started the next day! When you're doing what you really enjoy, you're not even aware of the passage of time. You become very focused, and what you produce tends to be very, very good. That can only enhance your chances of success.

Success Stories In Self-Publishing: Bestselling Authors Who Began As Self-Publishers

Independent publishers account for 70 percent of all book titles. But, the "big" publishers get $25 billion of a $40 billion market. Some estimates say that there may be as many as 100,000 small and self-publishers!

While we know about 100,000 book titles are published each year, we have no idea how many manuscripts are collectively written and submitted to publishers each year. Most publishers receive far more than ten manuscripts for each one they publish. Many big publishing houses receive hundreds, if not thousands, of manuscripts for each one they choose to publish.

The annual *Writer's Market* lists publishers receptive to new author titles. *Writer's Market* is also a valuable resource for locating places which buy serial rights, excerpts, and articles from your authors.

Because of the long-shot involved in getting a book published by a big publishing house, many authors self-publish their first book so they can establish a profitable track record of growing book sales. Then, they sell their title to a big publisher. Their goal is not to be a publisher as much as a celebrity author.

Some titles you might recognize that began life as self-published books: *What Color is Your Parachute?* by Richard Nelson Bolles; *ZAPP! The Lightning of Empowerment* by Bill Byham; *The Celestine Prophecy* by James Redfield; and *The One-Minute Manager* by Ken Blanchard and Spencer Johnson. Spencer Johnson went on to write the bestselling *Who Moved My Cheese?* which sold over ten million copies worldwide.

Just-In-Time Inventory: How Many Copies Should You Print?

For a first press run, you probably should only print 1,000 copies of a new book. You might even consider using the newer printing-on-demand (POD) capability which allows production runs of only a hundred books or so at a time. Many experienced, small publishers tend to agree with sticking to a small first press run.

New publishers are seduced into larger press runs because the larger press run leads to lower per unit production costs. For a 128-page 5X8 book, here are some older estimates:

Number Of Copies	Total Printing Cost	Cost Per Unit
1,000 copies	$1,763	$1.76
2,000 copies	$2,515	$1.26

At 1,000 copies, the cost per unit is $1.76. At 2,000 copies, the cost per unit is $1.26. The difference of $0.50 represents nearly a 30% increase in your per unit cost. That difference can seduce you into printing more books with a first press run.

However, it's important to realize that your first press run represents a test. Can you sell 1,000 copies of your book? Many small publishers are dismayed to find that they only sell a few hundred copies of their first book in their first year. Even for books featured on the *Tonight Show*, you might only sell a few hundred copies in your first year!

Some publishers tend to argue two points. First, if you go with the larger press run, extra books can be given away as complimentary marketing copies. So, in the above case, the second thousand books cost about $752 or a measly $0.75 per unit. Even if those books don't sell, they can be given away to book reviewers in an attempt to generate more publicity for your book. The hope is that the $752 extra dollars spent can be used to generate publicity.

However, this reasoning is somewhat flawed because a new book probably won't generate many reviews, and the review outlets are quite limited for any given topic. Remember, around 100,000 books are published each year and each of these books wants its share of publicity! Most of them get their fair share of publicity, which is very little! Mass mailing books into that great Book-Reviewer-Promotional-Ether isn't likely to garner reviews. What will probably happen is that any remaining inventory will sit around and consume space.

The second, and more valid, reason used to justify the larger press run is that you can keep the books in storage until they sell. Maybe it will take three years before they sell, but you'll still have a lower per unit cost and, hence, a greater profit per unit. That is very valid reasoning. However, there are two caveats you need to consider.

Caveat 1
What are the carrying costs of storing your books? Are your books stored adequately to prevent deterioration over a number of years?

If you anticipate storing your books in a climate-controlled house, then you can store your books for many, many years, and they will remain as new. But, if the books are stored under less than ideal conditions, for example, in a non-climate-controlled garage, there is danger that the books will absorb moisture over time. Be certain your books are properly stored if you plan to keep them for years. If you're keeping the books in your own building, house, or garage, you probably don't really have any 'carrying costs' for the books. 'Carrying costs' refer to the out-of-pocket costs you absorb just to keep the books in inventory. If a fulfillment company stores and ships your books, there might well be an annual per-unit or per-pallet charge for keeping books in inventory.

For example, Publishers Storage And Shipping (www.psscnj.com) charges about $140 a year per 1,000 books stored. You'll want to be sure that the extra savings of the larger press run isn't offset by this per-unit storage cost. When seeking a fulfillment company inquire into all fees you must pay. Request a rate schedule of all the company's fees.

In addition to per-unit storage costs, a fulfillment company might charge a flat annual fee or have an annual minimum that must be paid. This annual minimum can be about $500 regardless of fulfillment activity. So, if book storage fees and fulfillment fees only add up to $300 for the year, you'll be billed an extra $200. This is one reason why a small publisher often can't justify using a fulfillment agency until sales are in the thousands.

Caveat 2

In addition to inventory carrying costs, there is also 'opportunity cost.' Do you have other more profitable uses for the cash tied up in inventory?

The money tied up in inventory could be invested or used to produce other books. (For example, if you place $752 into stocks and they yield 10%, that's $75.20 in a year) Or, it could be used for more marketing to generate more sales.

If you self-publish and have plenty of money to produce more books, then 'opportunity cost' isn't a big issue. You'll have enough cash to produce your next book. But, if you're cash-strapped or if you're aggressively publishing other authors, that extra $752 can be used to produce another book. Maybe this other book will turn into a bestseller or an annual moneymaker! Getting the book out earlier has financial value to you!

Many people feel that inventory is a good thing. After all, inventory is an asset! But, another way to look at inventory is that it's an expense waiting to happen! The per-unit cost of a book in inventory will become part of cost-of-goods-sold (COGS), an expense. Not only is inventory an expense waiting to happen, but, something can devalue your inventory in the meantime. For example, maybe, you've written a book about Windows XP and Microsoft changes their operating system to Windows PP. Your Windows XP books would become outdated.

Just-In-Time Inventory

Many businesses use Just-In-Time Inventory. Just-In-Time Inventory is just what you'd expect—it's inventory that arrives just in time for you to sell it! That minimizes the amount of cash you need to tie up. Just-In-Time Inventory *often* leads to a higher return on your initial investment. Just-In-Time Inventory *always* minimizes your financial risk when publishing a book.

The key to successful inventory management is balancing the production costs with the carrying costs to determine the optimal reorder quantity—in our case, how many books should you print? We can derive mathematical formulas to determine optimal reorder points. But I don't think small publishers really need that level of detail!

As a rule, if you're using offset printing, you probably want to print at least 1,000 or 1,500 copies per press run. 2,000 is a nice number. If you're confident you can sell more, printing 3,000 per press run is a great amount. If you have an established sales history for a title, press runs of 5,000 are about the largest I'd recommend. Once you get up to press runs of about 5,000 copies, the per unit cost drops off so minutely that there really isn't any advantage to printing more copies. Only if you're fulfilling current demand, should you print more than 5,000 copies at a time.

Of course, there's always an exception to the rule. When, Kaye Thomas, author of *Consider Your Options*, joined the Publish-L mailing list as a new publisher, his first question was something like: "I don't know how many copies to print. Should I print 200,000 copies to get the benefit of better per-unit costs? Or, should I only print 50,000 to be conservative and safe?"

I'm all for optimism, but I don't want to see anyone get buried in unsaleable books! I suggested he limit his first press run to at most 5,000 copies. Turned out, Thomas had an established website, fairmark.com, which received a hundred thousand hits a month. And, his book was on a very timely topic—employee stock options. In the first nine months, he sold 25,000 copies. If you already have a *solid* following from a popular website, syndicated column, TV show, or something else, you *might* increase your press run to 5,000 copies.

Let's go back to our example:

Number Of Copies	Total Printing Cost	Cost Per Unit
1,000 copies	$1,763	$1.76
2,000 copies	$2,515	$1.26

While it appeared that we saved $0.50 per book by going with the larger press run, it's important to understand that the cost of producing a book consists of two very different parts. One part is the "Pre-Press," which includes the making of printing plates, for example. These are one-time costs. The other part consists of costs directly related to the number of units produced, for example, paper and printing cost. These costs increase directly with the number of units produced.

For the above estimates, suppose $600 represents one-time set up charges that vanish upon a reprint. Whenever you get quotes from printers always ask the printer to tell you how much of the cost is pre-press. Equivalently, how much would reprint costs be reduced if you reprinted the book? Suppose that you have two press runs of 1,000 copies. Rather than $3,526 (two times $1,763), the cost of two press runs might be $2,926.

So, while it looks like the 2,000 copy press run has a per unit cost of $1.26 and the 1,000 copy press run has a per unit cost of $1.76 making the savings $0.50 per unit, two 1,000 copy press runs together actually have a net per unit cost of $1.46. This represents only a 16% savings. And, given the uncertainty in sales for a new book, such a savings is not all that significant.

Change Is Good

You might not be happy with your book and want to make changes. You might decide you want changes made to the cover, for example. After a first press run, it is common for publishers to go back and add promotional blurbs to the back cover of a book or to the first few inside pages.

For example, if Oprah said your book was the best she ever read, that's something you want people to know! A reprint allows the option of making those changes and additions. For each book you publish, keep a small folder with one copy in it and a list of page numbers and changes you plan to make on a revision. Record all corrections. For small changes, you might decide not to make any changes on the next press run because of the extra set-up charges.

You Don't Need To Print All Your Books At Once!

Many new publishers feel that to sell 5,000 books in a year, they must initially print 5,000 books. This isn't true! There is no reason you can't have multiple press runs within a year! New publishers worry about not being able to keep up with demand if their book takes off. They fear they won't have enough money to reprint enough copies. However, you'll probably be able to produce more copies than you expect. This is due to the power of bootstrapping and compounding. Bootstrapping and compounding basically say you reinvest money earned from previous sales to finance larger levels of future sales.

A Book Riddle: The Power Of Reinvestment Of Earnings

Suppose your book costs $2 per unit to produce and earns $2 profit per unit sold. You have only $4,000 to produce books. Suppose that your books sell out immediately the first of the month and that your distributor pays you at the end of the month. Suppose the time to reprint is minimal and returns and taxes aren't an issue. How many copies can you afford to produce in your first year?

Don't you just hate word problems? The answer is that you can produce 8,192,000 books in the first year, and, at the end of January, the next year, your distributor sends you a nice check for a tad over $16 million dollars.

This is the power of compounding, bootstrapping, and the reinvestment of earnings! I devote an entire chapter to this topic in *Thinking Like An Entrepreneur: How To Make Intelligent Business Decisions That Will Lead To Success In Building And Growing Your Own Company.*

Let's work a slightly less challenging problem:

Suppose your book costs $2 per unit to produce and earns $2 profit per unit sold. You have only $4,000 to produce books. Suppose that your books sell out immediately the first of the month and that your distributor pays you every three months or four times a year. Suppose the time to reprint is minimal and returns and taxes aren't an issue. How many copies can you afford to produce in your first year?

Let's draw a line to represent one year and break the year into four equal periods.

2,000

At the start of the year, because we have $4,000 and the books cost $2 per unit, we can immediately produce 2,000 books. By assumption, the books sell immediately, and we earn $2 per unit profit. We also recover the initial investment of $2 per unit (Think of the money used to purchase inventory as an investment in the sense that the money is placed in inventory and an up-front cost is absorbed. Then, when the inventory sells, we recover our cost per unit and earn a profit per unit.). Thus, each book sold gives us $4.

But, our distributor doesn't pay us what we're owed immediately, so we must wait until the end of the first quarter to receive our money. The second tick on the line represents the end of the first quarter and the beginning of the second. At the second tick, we receive $8,000. And, we have enough to print 4,000 copies of our book, as we reinvest all the money into producing more books.

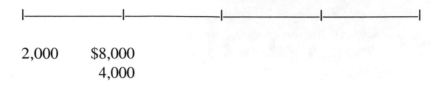

2,000 $8,000
             4,000

By assumption, we print the books immediately and they sell immediately. So, at Tick 2, we also sell all 4,000 copies produced. However, our distributor doesn't pay us until the end of the quarter, so we must wait until the third tick on the line to receive payment for 4,000 books. At the third tick (end of the second quarter), we receive $16,000. We immediately reinvest the $16,000 to produce 8,000 books. And, they sell immediately.

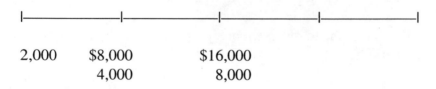

2,000 $8,000 $16,000
             4,000   8,000

It is now the end of the second quarter, and we've sold 8,000 books. But, we must wait until the fourth tick (end of the third quarter) to receive payment. At the fourth tick, we receive $32,000, and we immediately print 16,000 copies. And, they immediately sell! If only real-life publishing were this regular! The diagram below shows the situation:

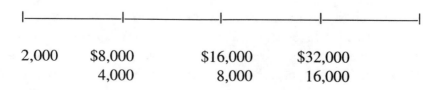

2,000 $8,000 $16,000 $32,000
             4,000   8,000   16,000

Finally, we immediately sell the 16,000 copies at the fourth tick, but, again, our distributor doesn't pay us until the end of the year, the fifth and final tick. When the year ends, the distributor sends us a check for $64,000.

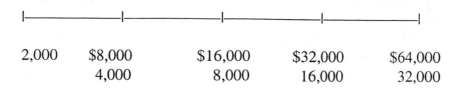

2,000	$8,000	$16,000	$32,000	$64,000
	4,000	8,000	16,000	32,000

Thus, at the end of the year, we collect $64,000 and can immediately produce 32,000 books. When those 32,000 books sell (we've actually just nudged into the second year), our distributor sends us a nice juicy check for $128,000 and we've sold 32,000 books. We must wait until the end of the first quarter *next year* to receive our money.

Remember that we only could afford to produce 2,000 books at the start of the year. Yet, within about a year, we were able to finance the sale of *32,000* books! This is the power of compounding at work. Money kept in a company and reinvested to grow profits can have a tremendous effect! If you want to read more brutal details about compounding, see *Thinking Like An Entrepreneur: How To Make Intelligent Business Decisions That Will Lead To Success In Building And Growing Your Own Company.*

The above analysis neglects three important factors. First, we will probably need to withdraw some of the profits during the year. If you're working really hard to build and grow a publishing company, and you don't have much money to begin with, you'll probably need to pay yourself a small salary to live. Of course, if you have another job or other sources of income this is best of all as you can reinvest more money until your sales are substantial. Also, as your sales grow, you'll typically have more money tied up in inventory and accounts receivable.

Second, you're earning excellent money, and the IRS will want some of that! Taxes will take a big bite out of how fast you can grow. You'll need to make estimated tax payments throughout the year, and taxes will consume some of your profits. You could work the above example assuming a given tax rate to see how taxes limit growth. For example, if you assume a net income tax rate of 37%, at the end of the first quarter, rather than having $4,000 from profits to reinvest, you'd have only $2,520 in profits to reinvest to produce more books. The other $1,480 would be sent to the IRS as an estimated tax payment.

Taxes are a unique 'expense' of operating a business in that you only pay taxes when you make money. If you fail to make money, you won't pay taxes. And, if you lose money and your company is a sole proprietorship or an S-Corporation, you'll probably be able to deduct the loss from your other income and save some tax money.

Because of the nature of taxation, many publishers seek profitable and tax deductible ways to reinvest money toward the end of the tax year. For example, advertising expense is tax deductible in the current tax period even though it benefits your company into the future.

Let's assume you contemplate an advertising campaign with a cost of $5,000. If you initiate this campaign before your current tax year ends, you absorb an expense of $5,000. Your taxable income is reduced by $5,000. If you had kept the $5,000 and waited until next year to initiate the advertising campaign, you'd be taxed on that $5,000. If your combined federal and state tax rate is 36%, you'd pay an extra $1,800 in taxes by not having the expense. That's $1,800 *less* you have to spend on advertising next year! We should note that this doesn't prevent taxation. It only *defers* your taxes for another year and allows your money to grow more rapidly because it's growing somewhat tax deferred. That reinvested $5,000 had better lead to recovering $5,000 and generating even more income, all of which will eventually be taxed!

The decision as to whether or not you should spend the $5,000 on the advertising campaign isn't influenced by tax concerns. If you expect the campaign will be profitable, you'd run it. If you think it won't be profitable, you wouldn't run it. Taxation concerns only affect the *optimal time* to run the campaign once you've decided that it's a good campaign to run.

Third, and most important, the above analysis simply shows how quickly sales *can* grow as a result of *reinvested earnings. It doesn't mean that you'll actually be able to make those sales*! Just because you have the money to finance a certain level of sales doesn't mean that those sales will, in fact, materialize! In reality, if you generate 16,000 sales of your book in your first year, you're doing exceptionally well!

You must really work to promote your books if you want explosive growth. I hope the above exercise has helped you understand the importance of reinvestment of earnings, compounding and growth in business. If you have profitable products and you *reinvest* to create more profitable products, you aren't nearly as limited as you might feel you are at the start of the venture. When you started, you were only able to produce 2,000 books. At the end of only a year, you could afford to produce a whopping 32,000 books!

What happens if you're exceptionally successful in generating sales of your new book to the point that you actually sell *more* than 32,000 copies within the first year? Using the above estimates, you would need to borrow money to produce more than 32,000 books within the year. Or you would need to put more of your own money into your company. Because banks won't typically lend small start-up companies money, personal savings and borrowing from friends and relatives are the typical sources of finance for a small publisher.

Notice that if you sell more than 4,000 books in the first quarter, you'd also run out of money. You'd need to find more money for a quick reprint or else you'd lose sales! Controlled growth is often better than explosive growth that gets out of control.

Selling Your Book To A Major Publishing House And Big Publisher Sales

Another option to deal with runaway sales would be to sell your book to a larger publisher and become an author who receives royalties for books sold. Larger publishers are eager to acquire books that have an outstanding sales record, because larger publishers often view each book launched as a test. They don't know if the book will be successful or not. And, they're looking for a few big winners to generate profits and offset their losers. By showing your book has an established track record, you've probably removed much of the risk for the big publisher.

With this in mind, be sure to ask for a significant advance! You probably won't beat the record advance of $4,125,000 paid to the author and self-publisher of *The Christmas Box*. But, advances between $10,000 and $250,000 are common for an established book. Remember, your book is already selling!

We should also point out that you want the royalty paid to you to be based upon the retail price of the book and not the net amount received by the publisher. Having a royalty based upon the net received by the publisher is much less valuable. Publishers often only receive 45% of a book's list price. So, royalties based on net to the publisher are less than half as valuable as royalties based upon full retail price. Unfortunately, for authors, more and more publishers are paying royalties based upon the net the publisher receives.

Also, examine the contract carefully. Consider some minimum guarantee of the financial effort the publisher will put into marketing. Remember, if you're spending $1 per book on marketing as a self-publisher, the large publisher might divert that money to promote another author's book.

You might also want to read a book about publishing contracts, such as *Kirsch's Guide to the Book Contract : For Authors, Publishers, Editors and Agents* by Jonathan Kirsch. Also, when you're dealing with such large amounts of money, having a lawyer examine the details of a contract is valuable.

Another thing that might help you gain a larger advance and better contract terms is auctioning off the rights to your book. Get more than one publisher interested and try to get multiple publishers bidding against one another. Many times, when a ridiculous amount of money is paid for something, it's because the thing was sold at an auction. People like to win and often become competitive when faced with competitors. This is why ugly lamps on eBay sell for $1,000. Many people who *win* auctions have winner's regret! After the excitement's over, they'd rather have their money than the lamp. For more about this, see *Influence: How and Why People Agree To Things* by Robert Cialdini.

Also, you might want to examine your contract to be sure there's a clause saying that if your book is taken out-of-print you regain all rights to your book. This would allow you to self-publish the book or take it to another publisher. Most publishers won't object to this clause because if they've taken your book out-of-print, they probably don't want anything more to do with it. Occasionally, out-of-print books are 'reissued.' But, as an author, you don't want to wait five years for your book to become available again!

While smaller publishers and self-publishers can make a profit on as few as 1,000 sales (or even less), major publishing houses must usually sell at least 5,000 copies before they generate a profit. This is because larger publishers have much larger overhead to cover, including salaries of administrative staff, building rents, forklift repair, etc. When they are starting, smaller publishers often work from their homes. And, they usually don't own a forklift. The difference between a small publisher and a mid-sized publisher is often a forklift and a building!

Dealing With Company Growth—Pallets, Forklifts, Book Storage, And Insurance

Notice that as your sales grew in our example, you went from selling 2,000 copies to selling 32,000 copies. Methods you adopt for lower sales levels might not work well for higher sales levels. This is true of everything from order flow and billing to inventory management and packing and shipping.

Suppose your books come 40 books to a case. Your first order of 2,000 books consisted of only 50 cases. A big truck pulled up in front of your house and the union driver said, "Go Get Your Books!" Dealing with union drivers is quite a topic in itself.

Anyway, you carried 50 cases inside and all is well. But, as sales grow, you'll quickly learn that handling your own books isn't a fun part of publishing. You'll want to hire employees or else outsource fulfillment.

At 32,000 books, you'd have 800 cases of books! You won't be thinking in terms of books, or even cases. You'll be thinking in terms of pallets! A pallet is a short, flat, wooden slab about four feet square that is designed so a forklift can pick it up.

Books from a large press run are typically placed into boxes. The boxes are stacked on pallets, and the boxes are shrink wrapped into one large bundle to keep them together in the event that the new forklift driver runs into a wall.

Always store your books on pallets and keep the books in their original boxes. Pallets keep the books several inches above the ground and allow air to circulate below the books. As you grow, to save space, you might want to stack your boxes of books higher. If you do this, buy some 4'x4' 1/4" thick boards to place on top of the pallets. This way the boxes sit on a completely flat and smooth surface.

Pallets often have large spaces between their boards. If you stack cases of books too high, the weight of the books can deform the cases on the bottom and possibly damage your books. The weight of the books will literally push the bottom boxes into the spaces between the boards of the pallet. You obviously don't want that! Don't overstack your cases.

Some publishers say they even elevate the pallet from the ground just a bit with a sheet of metal. Their idea is that concrete floors sweat, wooden pallets can absorb water from the concrete, and the cases could absorb water from the pallets. If you have decent climate control, this shouldn't be a problem. A wooden pallet on a concrete floor should be fine!

Many publishers run fans, dehumidifiers, or purchase Damp-Rid™ to prevent humidity from affecting books. Books should be stored in a dry and cool area.

Never store your books where water damage can occur. For example, never store books in a basement. The cardboard cartons can absorb moisture from the air even if water never touches the cartons.

Remember, too, that books are heavy. I've never heard of it happening, but I wouldn't be completely surprised to someday read about a successful self-publisher who tried to store 10,000 books in his second floor apartment or in his attic only to come home to find his floor collapsed!

This probably hasn't happened because successful small publishers quickly realize that happiness is the shortest distance between where the truck stops and where your books finally wind up being stored. For home-based self-publishers that usually means the garage. Many shippers charge extra for delivery to a private residence. Drivers want to be able to back the truck up to a loading dock, open the door, and have your forklift driver take it from there. They don't want to risk blowing out their back carrying your books.

That publisher with the hole in his floor would be in deep do-do! Homeowner's insurance typically doesn't protect business inventory. If you wish to insure your books, you'll probably need to add a rider to your homeowner's policy. This is true of business assets in general. Don't assume because your home is insured that your home-based business assets are also insured. Many fulfillment companies also require you to purchase insurance to cover the value of your inventory. Such insurance adds to the carrying costs of storing inventory.

Many small publishers don't insure their inventory. Many also don't purchase business interruption insurance. Personally, I'm not fond of inventory insurance. I'd rather just absorb the financial hit if need be. The real value in a book doesn't lie in inventory on hand. It rests in the ability to sell the title in the future. So your company could probably take a rare 'extraordinary' loss and survive. But, many publishers religiously insure their inventory.

For new small publishers, I don't recommend business interruption insurance. There usually isn't much of a business to 'interrupt' when you're starting! But, if your sales are substantial, in addition to insuring your inventory, you might want to estimate the loss involved if your company didn't have any books to sell for a month and consider business interruption insurance. Again, don't worry about this when you're just starting.

You won't be storing 32,000 books in your home. Don't even think it! You'll need a building. One problem of company growth is that overhead starts creeping in. Things you once ignored because you did them in a time-intensive fashion become expenses paid for as wages to others or as overhead in some form or another. Always try to plan ahead as you build your company. Be sure your books are sufficiently highly priced to allow for the eventual overhead that slowly creeps in.

Many savvy publishers realize that outsourcing fulfillment of book orders is a great option. Just because you sell 100,000 books a year doesn't mean you need to lift any of those books! Nor do you need a warehouse to store your books! And you don't need employees to lift those darn books!

Just-In-Time Distributor Payments

Notice the crucial importance of how frequently you're paid by your distributor in our previous example. We assumed quarterly payments. This put a real limitation on how quickly your company could grow by bootstrapping. Cash flow is a constant problem in the book publishing industry, and many publishers hold a hard and fast line of demanding prepayment for orders.

Cash flow problems arise because, even if a company is earning excellent profits on its products, payment is delayed. *Thinking Like An Entrepreneur: How To Make Intelligent Business Decisions That Will Lead To Success In Building And Growing Your Own Company* has a discussion of cash flow and how it influences business.

Unfortunately, if you try to demand prepayments from some of the biggest distributors, they'll look at you as if you're a bug from another planet. So, you'll need to realize that just because you sold 200 books to your distributor doesn't mean you'll receive payment right away. In fact, it probably will come several months later.

Other distributors seem to have payment cycles that are probably measured in centuries. It's as if book distributors were founded by Galapagos turtles. They seem to measure in turtle years.

You must draw a line in the sand beyond 90 days payment terms. Don't settle for 180 days or more! That's half a year! There's absolutely no reason on earth for anyone to hold your money that long. It's not only a serious hindrance to growth, but the longer you wait to collect payment, the more likely you won't ever collect anything. Distributors do go bankrupt and leave publishers with large unpaid bills. Ideally, there isn't any reason a bookseller or distributor can't pay within 30 days date of invoice which is common to many other industries.

In our example, we also assumed that reprints happened quickly. Reprints will often take a couple of weeks to a month or longer. You should ask your printer how quickly they can reprint your book. Popular printers must fit your reprint into their work schedule.

Be sure you reprint soon enough to prevent running completely out of copies. You don't want to receive individual orders you can't fulfill! As your company grows, establish trade credit with your printers. This means that you'll pay them within 30 days (or whatever terms you agree to) of having your books printed and invoiced to you.

Printing On Demand (POD)

Just-In-Time Inventory can be realized today for small publishers through Printing-On-Demand (POD) technology. Printing on demand uses newer technology to produce books in short press runs.

It's important to select your POD printer carefully. Thomson-Shore is one printer who tends to do an excellent job with POD printing as well as with larger run offset printing, though they are a bit more expensive than some other printers.

As with all printing jobs, get quotes from multiple printers. Post a question about any company you anticipate doing business with to a small publisher list, such as Publish-L. Ask if others have worked with the company and if they'd recommend using them. Overall, was their experience good or bad? Would they use them again? Were there any problems and was the quality of the printing adequate?

I've seen some POD books that looked as if they were produced on a copy machine, which is clearly inadequate. I've also seen other POD books that had excellent text printing and paper quality for inside pages, but which had covers which were too thin.

If the cover of a softcover book is too thin, it will tend to curl with time and use. Heat can also curl a thin book cover. That's one reason softcover books shouldn't be stored in hot locations. The uncoated side of the cover and the coated side of the cover respond differently to changing atmospheric conditions. The result can be a curled cover.

Ask any POD printer you contemplate using to send you a sample book. Open it. Read a bit of it. Examine the print quality, paper quality, binding quality (to be sure pages won't come out!), cover stock quality, etc. A well-produced POD book should be nearly indistinguishable from a book printed with traditional offset printing.

Ingram Lightning Source POD

Ingram, the powerhouse distributor, which distributes 175 million books annually, has a POD program called Lightning Source (www.lightningsource.com), which is a subsidiary company of Ingram.

The nice thing about Lightning Source is that they distribute your POD book through Ingram. Thus, if a bookstore places an order for your book with Ingram and Ingram orders from Lightning Source, your book is printed and sent to Ingram. Ingram then fills the bookstore order. You receive the wholesale price of the book less the printing cost. Thus, it's possible to sell a large number of books through Ingram without ever having to touch a book or pay in-bound shipping charges from a printer to your company.

The costs for Lightning Source vary. Lightning Source also offers drop shipping as an option. Drop shipping allows you to receive a customer order, forward the order to Lightning Source, and have Lightning Source fulfill the order.

Lightning Source prints in many sizes: 5X8, 6X9, 7.5X9.25, 8.25X11, etc. While you must check current costs for any printer, at the time of this writing, the first three sizes have a cost per unit of $0.90 for the cover plus $0.013 per page for each page in the book. There is also a minimal set-up fee to get the title into Lightning's database.

So, to produce a 256-page book would cost:

$0.90 + (256 \text{ x } \$0.013) = \$4.23$ per copy.

The drop ship option costs $1.75 for the first copy and $0.25 for each additional copy to the same address.

Let's work some examples. Suppose you sell a 200-page, 6x9 book for $19.95. You give distributors a 55% discount, which means you receive 45% of the retail price for each copy sold as your wholesale price.

For each copy sold, after allowing for the wholesale discount of 55%, you receive $8.97. The cost to produce each book is:

$$\$0.90 + (200 \times \$0.013) = \$3.50 \text{ per copy.}$$

Thus, with each copy Ingram sells directly to bookstores through Lightning Source, you receive $5.47 per copy. While that's excellent for modest sales and the convenience is nice, the per-unit cost per book is still higher than with offset printing. So, if you find you're selling 5,000 copies or more a year, you'll probably want to use regular offset printing and work through a fulfillment company to fulfill orders rather than absorb higher per unit POD costs. That offers the same 'turn-key' solution to order fulfillment while allowing you to earn a bit more money.

For the drop shipping option, rather than charging $0.013 per page, for some mysterious reason, Lightning Source charges $0.014 per page. So, the cost to produce your book is $3.70 per copy.

So, if a customer orders directly from your website and pays full retail price, for example, and you have Lightning Source drop ship the book, Lightning Source charges you $3.70 plus $1.75 plus actual postage, which we'll assume is $1.42 which is the lowest media mail rate. Thus, you receive $19.95 from the customer, plus whatever shipping you charge, if any. We'll assume you don't charge for shipping. And, you pay Lightning Source a total of $6.87. Thus, per book you 'earn' $13.08.

The great thing about the above option is that you never needed to actually handle the book. As a small publisher, it's best if you don't have to pack and ship books. That way your time can be used to develop new products and promote your existing books. Hiring an assistant to pack and ship books is also an option. But, then you must deal with management and employment issues.

However, if you want to earn a bit more money with each sale and you don't mind packing books yourself, you could have Lightning Source send you the books and you can pack and ship the individual orders yourself. You can have Lightning Source produce press runs of 25 copies, 100 copies, 200 copies, or whatever, and have them sent to you.

Replica Books And iUniverse.com

Other POD options include Baker & Taylor's Replica Books (www.replicabooks.com) and iUniverse.com. These programs work differently from Ingram's Lightning program. Replica Books serves as a *publisher*, and they acquire reprint rights to your book. Baker & Taylor promotes their service as a way of putting out-of-print titles back in print.

I'm not too familiar with iUniverse.com. They seem more geared to authors than publishers. They also serve as a book *publisher*, rather than as a pure POD printer.

Many new POD printers are also adequate for producing 'galley' copies of your book to send to 'prepublication' book reviewers. These review sources want copies of your book three months in advance of your publication date.

For marketing purposes, you'll probably want to have some copies on hand to send to book reviewers, columnists, radio and TV show producers, etc. With these copies, you'll probably want to include a special note and promotional information specific to the individual.

One key to successful operations in running a small book publishing company is choosing the right size press run and the right option for order fulfillment. Evaluate how much it costs you to produce each copy of your book and how much it costs to have book orders filled. Try to keep your inventory turnover high.

Book Marketing

Book marketing is the heart and sole of building a financially successful publishing company. By and large, marketing is what determines success. The most important questions you should ask are: How will I market my books? How will I generate sales? Who will want to buy my titles and why? Who is my niche and how do I reach them? How do other publishers successfully market their titles? Many successful publishers make it a point to do at least three things *every day* to market their books. Each day, ask yourself, "What have I done to market my books today?"

Write those questions down on a piece of paper and work to find answers. I'm not going to tell you there are hard and fast answers that will solve those problems. Too many new publishers have been unsuccessful in book marketing. But, hopefully, if you work hard, you'll sell your share of books and learn as you go.

Direct Mail. Just Say "No."

If you pick up a book about self-publishing, you're likely to encounter a chapter about using direct mail to sell books to individual customers. I don't really know why. Direct mail almost never works for self-published books.

While you can read about list testing, writing direct mail copy, bulk rate mail, and all the other fun aspects of direct mail, the reality is that direct mail is very expensive and the great majority of books lack sufficient profitability per unit to justify direct mail.

Today, direct mail costs about $60 to reach 100 people effectively. That's the marketing cost. If you achieve a 2% response, you're doing well. So, you might hope to sell two books per 100 direct mail letters sent out. That means each book, after all other expenses, had better offer a profit per unit of at least $30. Most books don't offer that much profit per book.

If you produce higher-priced books, then, you might want to test direct mail to very targeted lists. If you've published many related books and have a full catalog to offer, you might want to consider producing a catalog that can be mailed to customers and potential customers.

Another lower-cost option is to send out a less expensive postcard in an attempt to market your book. I don't believe these postcards are very effective. If you pay attention to the direct mail you receive as a potential customer, you'll notice that very little direct mail promoting books arrives in your mailbox. Established publishers know that direct mail is usually not effective given today's mailing costs.

Whenever you contemplate using a marketing strategy, look around for other companies doing the same thing. If you see many similar companies marketing through a particular marketing channel and they continue doing so, the marketing channel is probably effective. While you can pioneer new marketing methods, also consider doing what other publishers have found to be effective.

Don't be mislead by outdated stories telling you how one million books were sold by direct mail to individual consumers and how the author became rich in the process. The reality is that it doesn't happen today. Not for most small publishers, anyway.

Some publishers use direct mail to reach bookstores and libraries. Direct mail can be effective for more expensive products. Direct mail can also be effective if there is a high potential for repeat customer business. Book clubs use direct mail. But, they aren't selling one or two books.

Rather, they're selling a *membership*. Direct mail can be used because each customer is expected to buy many books while they remain in the book club. The value of the membership to the club is the estimated profit that the person yields by purchasing multiple books over several years. This is why book clubs send out direct mail offering, "Take three books for free and join our club!" That's very different from a small publisher using direct mail to sell one or two titles.

In addition to repeat business, book clubs are also in the marketing business. They often rent their customer lists to other businesses which can effectively use direct mail because they offer more expensive products. Many targeted customer lists rent for $30 per 1,000 names for a one-time mailing. That's a strong profit driver. All the members of a topic-specific book club represent a very targeted audience.

Other higher-priced products can be marketed by direct mail. Higher-priced newsletters are often promoted by direct mail. For example, investment newsletters often charge $120 or more for an annual subscription. Clearly, each sale offers upwards of $30 profit per unit and also the potential for renewals. However, if you plan to sell high-end newsletters, you need to offer valuable, specialized advice. General commentary usually won't do.

Consider magazine subscriptions. Magazines often use direct mail and offer annual subscriptions for $14 or some other ridiculously low price. The quality of the magazine's content is often very high. However, don't forget that the primary profit driver behind a magazine is advertising revenue. And, the more targeted readers a magazine reaches, the more it can charge its advertisers. So the price of the magazine subscription isn't nearly as important. The key is to have a large readership so that advertisers of cars and other expensive products will wish to advertise. Magazines also offer renewal potential and the opportunity to rent customer lists.

In addition to higher-priced newsletters, sometimes 'courses' are offered by direct mail. For some reason people are willing to pay more for a 'course' than for a 'book.' People tend to have preconceived ideas of what 'books' and 'courses' cost.

Yet, often 'courses' are books in disguise. Often, 'courses' are even cheaper to produce than books and can be created on an as-needed basis. This is because the 'course' consists of regular sheet paper punched and held together with a three-ring binder.

If you decide to produce a course, it's important to offer valuable information that is also rather specific and, hopefully, somewhat difficult to acquire by other means. Unfortunately, some companies produce high-end courses that really aren't worth the price.

One popular magazine for entrepreneurs offered three-ring binder courses for about $60 that told people how to build very specific businesses, such as a newsletter business. However, when I examined one of their courses, it seemed that 95% (or more) of the information was just basic information about starting any old business. The other 5% (or less) of the information was somewhat targeted, but commonly available. The only thing I found of value was a short list of a few trade associations, which could provide more specific information about starting a business in the particular industry.

Those types of 'courses' always annoy me, because it just doesn't seem that the added price is justified by a slight attempt to 'specialize' the information. But, it does illustrate the concept that if you can start with a core of information and then differentiate it in different directions, you can charge substantially more for the information. If you're thinking of starting a dry-cleaning company, for example, which title appeals to you more:

A 'book': "How To Start Your Own Business" ?
Or, a 'course': "How To Start Your Own Dry Cleaning Company" ?

But, someone thinking of starting an accounting practice will probably favor the first title. So, by specializing, even as more money is charged for the material, a narrower niche is reached.

If you do a little more research, add some useful information specific to running an accounting business, you could launch another 'course' called "How To Start Your Own Accounting Practice." And, so on and so on.

While you could imagine doing this for a three-ring binder course as a way of diversifying and specializing a product line within a niche (the niche of people starting businesses), you can use the same marketing approach for conventional books.

The key is that the magazine offering these courses was already targeted to people interested in starting a business. By specializing each 'course' within that niche, the magazine could charge *more for the course and, at the same time, probably create a higher likelihood of generating a sale*, because the targeted content would be more appealing to someone thinking of starting that specific business.

Once you are effectively marketing to a niche, think about how you can more profitably reach into that niche by even more specialization.

While I'm not impressed with adding minimally specialized information and charging a bundle for it, as a publisher of other books, you could use this principle to decide what kind of books to publish. Once you develop expertise in marketing to a particular niche, you might want to consider producing *related* titles.

In addition to courses and newsletters, publishers can also use direct mail to promote speaking engagements and seminars. Direct mail response rates for seminars are usually low, but the seminar price is relatively high. If you're interested in learning more about the seminar business, I recommend *Marketing And Promoting Your Own Seminars And Workshops* by Fred Gleeck.

If you want to learn more about direct mail, I recommend *Profitable Direct Marketing* by Jim Cobs and *Successful Direct Marketing Methods* by Bob Stone.

More About Titles

Naming your title is an important part of marketing. Consider the two title comparison:

"How To Start Your Own Business"
"How to Start Your Own Dry Cleaning Company"

Each title conveys slightly different information. One is more specific. As a general rule, when you name your books, you want the titles to be specific enough to tell the reader what the book is about.

And, the titles should to be clever enough to interest potential reviewers and others who might be able to promote your book.

Fun books should have fun titles. Serious books probably need more serious titles.

When I published my first book, *Thinking Like An Entrepreneur*, I thought the title was great. People are interested in becoming entrepreneurs, and the title made it clear that the book was for people who wanted to learn to think like entrepreneurs.

Unfortunately, I later learned (see InfluenceAtWork.com) that people, as a general rule, really don't like to think. Thinking is too much work. In most people the brain waves created by engaging in difficult thinking mirrors the pain-inducing brain waves of people who have their hand thrust into ice-cold water. Bummer. I did not know that when I named my first book!

For my second title, I selected *Becoming An Investor: Building Wealth By Investing In Stocks, Bonds, And Mutual Funds* rather than *Thinking Like An Investor*. "Becoming" sounds easier than "Thinking."

Many publishers test titles. If one title doesn't work, they rename the book and see if it does better with a different title. Sometimes, people will claim the difference in a book's performance is due entirely to a newer and better title. That's always difficult to know.

Usually, when a renamed book comes out, the book receives a whole slew of new promotion. So, it's not always clear that Title XXX outsold Title YYY by twelve copies to two million copies due to a better title. There are too many other factors at work to claim a difference in success is mostly due to the title.

Bounce your title ideas around with your friends, family, and other authors and publishers. On publisher lists, a common question is, "What do you think of my title? Any other title and subtitle ideas?"

On Publish-L, I recall Kaye Thomas posting that question for his book on stock options. He had a pretty lame and boring title. Along with other publishers, I suggested some other titles, including my share of lame ones. I did come up with one title I thought was rather clever: "Getting Your Share: The Employee's Guide To Equity Compensation."

I thought that double meaning was cute, yet the title conveyed the book's content. I also pointed out that titles that start with the first few letters of the alphabet are better because they tend to be shown first in many lists of books. At the time, for example, amazon.com displayed titles in alphabetical order. Today, amazon usually displays titles in bestselling or featured-title order by default. I don't like titles that start with numbers because I think many people just bypass those titles.

Kaye outdid me and came back with the title, *Consider Your Options*, which was great. It also had that clever duality. Brainstorming title ideas often helps publishers. So, don't hesitate to get title feedback.

Of course, some authors choose titles that aren't particularly descriptive of the content of their books and do well. Harvey Mackay felt confident that *Swim With The Sharks Without Being Eaten Alive* was right for his first book, despite the publisher hating the title.

The publisher felt people would think it was a scuba diving book or something like that. But, Mackay turned out to be right, and his books have sold over six million copies worldwide. Of course, Mackay is one of the world's greatest public speakers and a humorous and knowledgeable business writer, so he probably would have done well with any reasonably good title.

I mention Mackay's book, because back when he was the only one who liked his title, he had a survey taken to determine if other people would like the title and understand what the book was about. And, the survey showed they did.

While survey results can be speculative and can be manipulated to show almost anything, if you plan to spend bundles of money on marketing a new book, you might want to consider having a survey taken to see if potential readers like the title and to compare your proposed title with some alternatives.

Of course, statistical testing of book titles is rather extreme. Most small publishers instinctively choose a title they like and run with it. That's probably the best course of action.

Carried to its logical conclusion, we could imagine testing everything in a book. Do readers like the title? Do they like the story?

Do they like the ending? Then, we could cut out anything readers don't like in an attempt to make the book more marketable. But, as small publishers do we really want to do this?

Testing is common in the movie industry where millions of dollars are at stake. Test audiences sit watching pre-releases of movies and clicking little boxes which tell the movie producers what the viewers like and dislike about the film. Discussions, analysis, and editing follow in an attempt to make the movie more appealing to audiences.

In *Fatal Attraction* the original ending had the troubled Glenn Close character committing suicide. But, audiences *hated* that ending. Suddenly, they felt bad for Close. They blamed Michael Douglas for getting involved with her and dumping her. Suddenly, the ending wasn't clear, but murky. So, the ending was rewritten to have Close attempt to kill the Douglas character, absolving him of blame.

The lesson is that market testing permeates our lives. As publishers, we want to be aware of it, even if we decide not to use it. Many things we take for granted can be tested. And, ultimately, from a marketing standpoint, it's important to remember that what we like isn't as important as what the customer likes. When, in doubt, ask yourself if there is a way to test your marketing idea.

Keywords In Titles

While the ranking of your title in alphabetical order relative to similar books isn't crucial today, it's important to note that if a person goes to an online bookstore, such as amazon.com, and searches for a keyword or phrase and if your book contains that keyword or phrase within the first 15 words or so of the title, there's a greater chance that your book will be displayed in the returned results. So, give some thought to what keywords should be in your book's title. What terms will your readers search for when looking for information covered by your book?

In addition, the publishing industry uses many classification systems to categorize books. The Library of Congress Subject Headings is the most common one. Many searches return titles that match keywords in the title's LC subject headings. Subject headings are listed in a five-volume manual called *Library of Congress Subject Headings* ("the big red books" or LCSH) which is available at many public libraries.

Classifying your titles properly helps the marketing effort. Suppose you've written a book about a particular topic, for example, cooking with vegetables. If a person searches for 'cookbooks' or 'diet cookbooks' or any other phrase which is appropriate to your book, you want your book to be listed in the results returned by the search. People can only buy books they know about!

Success Begets Success

Success begets success, when it comes to book sales. Once a book hits the bestseller lists, those lists are widely distributed to newspapers throughout the country. And, many people see those bestseller lists and might choose to buy some of the books listed. Thus, a book that makes it to the bestseller lists has a powerful advantage to remain a bestseller! Eventually, newer books will overtake current bestsellers in popularity and drive them out of the top slots.

Getting onto the bestseller lists is the only snag! But, remember, in publishing, success can often snowball. What determines whether a book will really take off and do spectacularly well?

Many people have tried to answer that question. Probably one of the better books for learning how trends start is *The Tipping Point: How Little Things Can Make A Big Difference* by Malcolm Gladwell.

Gladwell argues word-of-mouth trends start when people he calls 'connectors' and 'mavens' adopt a product or service and tell other people about it. Connectors have diverse social networks and so have significant ability to spread information.

Mavens tend to habitually recommend great products. Further, your message must be 'sticky,' meaning that readers will remember your message.

Most experienced authors and publishers will tell you they haven't a clue what really causes some books to take off like a rocket—for example, the Harry Potter series for children, which I believe sold over 100 million copies—while other books sell only a few copies and die an unpopular death.

You want to get copies of your titles into the hands of key influential people who are positioned to promote your book. For example, if you write a how-to book, get copies of your book to syndicated, how-to writers.

Before Oprah Winfrey closed her book club, a favorable mention from Oprah typically sold 600,000 copies! One egotistical, Minnesota author felt his work was too good to have Oprah's book club sticker on his book, and a short while later, Oprah closed her club. Find media celebrities who influence millions and who might enjoy and recommend your book.

Syndicated writers and certain newspapers are very effective publicity outlets. In particular, The Associated Press (www.ap.org) picks up articles from a few key newspapers and distributes those articles to many other newspapers. So, if you happen to get featured in one of those newspapers, you might see your feature appear in newspapers throughout the country. Notice what other newspapers serve as a supplementary source of stories and news for your local paper to see what newspapers are picked up by The Associated Press.

To locate other newspapers and publicity outlets, check with your local library for directories of newspapers, magazines, TV, and radio programs.

The Standard Periodical Directory is one popular source. Most local libraries have several directories, and your librarian is your best source of information here. Just tell him or her you're looking for a directory of newspapers, or whatever else you want. Many of these publications are quite pricey, so I'd save several hundred dollars by using a library. In addition to your local public library, university libraries have many directory publications.

Influence

Robert Cialdini's book, *Influence: How and Why People Agree To Things*, is very good reading for book promoters. *Influence* helps us understand marketing by understanding how people are influenced. Cialdini has devoted his life to understanding how influence works.

Two key factors mentioned by Cialdini are especially relevant to book promotion. Cialdini shows us that "social proof" is an important factor of influence. Cialdini argues that only 5% of people are leaders, while 95% of people are followers. And, as previously mentioned, many people don't like to think.

So, to avoid the difficult work of thinking for themselves, many people look to others to determine correct behavior in social situations. There is an implicit assumption by many people that what is popular must be correct or good. This is why bestselling books always promote themselves as 'bestselling' books. Frequently, you'll see the number of copies sold printed on the cover.

For example, the cover of *Influence* reads, "Over 200,000 copies sold!" Often, the number is surrounded by a gold star or something else to draw attention to the fact. The popular *For Dummies*™ sequence of books proclaims, "Over 24 Million *For Dummies*™ Books In Print."

You never see a gold star boasting, "One Million Copies In Print! 990,000 still in the warehouse!" or "200 copies sold worldwide!" Popularity sells. The implicit assumption is that a million readers can't be wrong.

Sometimes, when popularity doesn't exist, some nefarious publishers have tried to create the illusion of popularity. This is equivalent to faith healers placing comrades in the audience to jump up and say they were cured.

I've been told that, in the past, employees of some big name publishers went to various local bookstores to buy copies of certain books to help the books make the bestseller lists. Apparently, this 'priming the pump' worked.

However, small publishers don't need to worry about the ethical dilemma of using such methods. Small publishers don't have the buying clout to achieve bestseller status by buying their own books!

However, you might want to drop into a local bookstore and try to order your book for an entirely different reason. You want to be sure that your book is listed as available. Surprisingly, even if your book is distributed by the big distributors, many bookstores might still show no record of availability of your book. Rather than just trust what your distributor says, the best confirmation of 'availability' is to test it yourself. Because of the cost, you should only do this when you suspect that your title isn't listed correctly. Ask your bookseller if they can check their distributor databases to see if they have access to your book.

Amazon rankings are another example of 'social proof' at work. Amazon ranks books in bestselling order. So, if you have two books, one of which is ranked at 100 and the other at 980,000, many readers will assume that the higher selling book is a better book. After all, no one else is reading the poorer-selling book.

Just as getting on print publication bestseller lists helps sell more books, getting a high ranking at Amazon helps sell more books on amazon.com, because Amazon regularly makes lists of books available in bestselling order.

So, if you write a book about cooking and it makes the top one hundred cooking books at amazon.com, many people will learn about your book because it's listed more frequently at Amazon. Typically, Amazon displays the top 25 or top 50 books in a category on the first page of returned results, so getting into the top 50 is particularly desirable. Amazon also features popular books in e-mail newsletters.

Incidentally, many authors check the rankings of their books almost daily. I'd try not to do that after you publish your first book or it could become an addiction. And I don't know of any support groups for authors who compulsively check their amazon rankings but who want to get rid of that time-consuming habit.

Amazon is unique in that it also offers some other ways to get your book listed and displayed, even if your book isn't among the top 50 selling books in its category. For example, amazon currently allows people to create 'listmania' lists, 'So, you want to...?' guides, and reader reviews.

Amazon Listmania lists allow you to create a list of books and give your list a title. Then, if viewers at amazon search for a topic related to the keywords in your list or related to the topics of the books mentioned in your list, there's a chance that your listmania list will display. Link to your own books in addition to other titles, of course. This is a great way to get some free publicity.

Even the renown sports marketer Jon Spoelstra, author of *Marketing Outrageously: How to Increase Your Revenue by Staggering Amounts*, has created listmania lists for his book.

Amazon "So, you want to" guides are similar. Readers can give people advice on various topics and link to books and other products with their guides. The guides also display at Amazon when readers search for keywords in the guide title or for subjects related to the mentioned books.

Amazon reader reviews probably aren't as useful from a pure marketing standpoint as listmania lists and "So, you want to" guides. But, Amazon allows readers to review books. If the review is clearly just self-promotional, Amazon will delete the review, but Amazon allows reviewers to include a brief line mentioning that they are the author of so-and-so. If you review titles related to your title, people reading about those titles might be alerted to your title's existence.

I enjoy reading other people's books and sharing my thoughts about their ideas and observations, so I've written quite a few book reviews on Amazon. In fact, I have a website, www.entrepreneurbooks.com, which has my reviews of small business, investing, personal finance, and self-help books.

The difficulty with writing reviews from a promotional standpoint is that so many people review the popular books on Amazon that each review is quickly pushed to the back pages where few readers see them. Add to that the time it takes to write a quality review, and you can see these reviews aren't particularly productive uses of a marketer's time.

In addition to reviewing related books, many publishers actively seek reader reviews on amazon.com for their own books. The common consensus among publishers I know is that reader reviews sell books. So, many publishers see who has reviewed similar books, contact them, and ask them if they'd like a free copy for possible review. Amazon also ranks their reviewers, so you can easily learn about the top reviewers who might be interested in the topic of your book.

Of course, some people ask friends and relatives to review their books. That's always seemed like cheating to me, so I've never done it. Other publishers and authors get e-mails or letters from readers who say they've enjoyed reading their book. Many publishers send a thank-you response and also mention that a positive review on amazon.com would be appreciated.

The downside to reader reviews on Amazon is that, occasionally, someone with a vendetta against you will try to attack you through an anonymous review that attacks your book. If it's clear the person probably hasn't read the book and only wants to attack you personally, you can request that Amazon remove the review, and they often will. Authors of controversial topics often have such reviews. Of course, if you write about a controversial topic, any discussion about your book is probably good.

Another factor of influence is 'authority.' We tend to trust people in positions of authority. Authority can stem from either a person's position or reputation. If you examine the back covers of books, you'll often see quotes praising the book from famous or semi-famous people. This is the authority factor being used to promote books.

To get authoritative reviews and positive comments about your book, get copies of your book to key people dealing with the topic of your book. For example, syndicated columnists who write about your topic should receive copies. Think about how you can reach key influential people who could mention your book favorably.

The highlight of favorable mentions for my book, *Thinking Like An Entrepreneur*, was when syndicated small business columnist Paul Tulenko (www.tulenko.com) reviewed *Thinking Like An Entrepreneur* and said: "One of the best all-around books for entrepreneurs I've read in a long time.... Buy this one, and wear it out."

I had been a long-time reader of Paul's small business column and greatly respected his knowledge, so that review meant a lot to me. One of the pleasures of writing is the ego boost of having knowledgeable people enjoy your book.

How To Select Authors

Paul Tulenko is publishing his own book about marketing, *Get More Business Right Now! Tools & Ammunition Designed To Fight Off The Alligators And Get The Business You Need!* I think Paul will be very successful with his book because he already has a tremendous following of business readers who love his column and because he's an established public speaker who teaches many people about entrepreneurship.

If your company decides to go beyond self-publishing and publish other authors, you want to consider the promotability of your authors as one factor in selecting authors to publish. While you always want to publish quality books, editors can always redo a book and make less-than-great writing pretty good. And, you might be able to add a coauthor to a book who has some real writing talent to make a book much more readable. *But, you can't make a person who isn't a natural book promoter into a book promoter.*

One of my favorite career books is *Now, Discover Your Strengths* by Marcus Buckingham and Donald Clifton. The authors argue that society is too focused upon trying to 'correct' people's weaknesses and make them well-rounded. Buckingham and Clifton argue that successful living and career success must follow from building upon your *natural strengths* and not trying to shore-up your weaknesses. I agree completely.

In particular, Buckingham and Clifton note that career success isn't the result of only a few actions. Rather, it's the result of your *many spontaneous day-to-day actions*. Your natural proclivities will dominate and determine whether you succeed or fail in a given career role. Certain natural strengths will benefit certain career roles. For example, if a person lacks a strength in 'analytical,' that person probably wouldn't make a great scientist.

Buckingham and Clifton tell us one of the natural strengths that some people posses is "wooer," which represents a natural tendency to get to know other people. To introduce yourself. Wooers tend to be friendly and outgoing. My mom is a natural "wooer." If she stands in a grocery store line for five minutes, she knows the life history of the people standing in front of her and behind her. And, they know hers.

I'm more anti-wooer. "Woo" is a natural strength that I believe is valuable for book promoters. People who enjoy public speaking and talking to others at every chance are more likely to mention they're an author and mention a book or two they've written. Added up every day of the year, the difference between a "wooer" promoting a book naturally and an introvert not promoting a book can make a big difference.

You might want to consider the natural strengths of your potential authors. Are they going to do a good job of *promoting* their titles? I know of an academic publisher who published a very well-written academic book. But, the author thought book promotion was beneath him. It was too commercial, and he didn't want to do it. Why publish an author who's going to make selling books difficult?

If you have a truly problematic author, you can always let the book go 'out-of-print.'

As a small publisher, you probably won't be able to attract the super-wooers, such as Bill Clinton, who command $10 million advances from large publishers. Celebrities are well-positioned to market their books, and that's a bigger factor in selecting which books get published than the quality of the writing.

Selecting Topics For Publication

If you publish other authors, you want to give strong consideration to the subjects you want to publish.

Many successful publishers focus upon only one particular niche, which they try to dominate. O'Reilly™ (www.oreilly.com) comes to mind. They publish many quality books about Unix, Linux, network administration, and related computer topics. Many network administrators have five or ten O'Reilly titles on their bookshelves. And each O'Reilly book tends to mention several other O'Reilly titles.

So, if you need to learn about the vi text editor (unless you're a masochist, you don't!) and you've read *Learning the vi Editor* by O'Reilly, that book will introduce you to other related Unix books. Mentioning your other related titles in the back of your books is a good example of free promotion. Each book becomes not only a source of profit, but a source of *promotion* if your titles are closely related.

Some topics are much easier to promote than other topics. Always contemplate the potential market for a particular title before deciding to publish it. Is the market large enough to justify your time and effort in editing and designing the book? Can you reach that market?

There are two very different schools of thought about topic selection. Some publishers like to find a topic that isn't already covered by many competitors' books and feel that being one of the first titles on the topic will be an edge. Other publishers look for an established market with many bestselling books in the area already. The theory is that a bestselling area will offer newer books the opportunity to squeeze in and capture sales about an already popular topic. You can always examine bestselling titles on Amazon to see what's selling.

Mini Case Study—Selling 100,000 Cookbooks A Year

I highly recommend new publishers read Suzanne Thomas's book *Make Money Self-Publishing: Learn How From Fourteen Successful Small Publishers* to gain insight from other publishers. One of the authors featured by Thomas is Bob Hoffman, who represents one of the most knowledgeable publishers I've had the honor of learning from via the Publish-L discussion list. Hoffman's story is a great mini-case study because of his knowledgeable marketing and business savvy.

Thomas tells us that Virginia and Bob Hoffman of the Hoffman Press (www.foodandwinebooks.com) wanted a hobby during their retirement years, so they decided to self-publish a book about cooking with wine.

clever

The Hoffman Press's success, Thomas explains, was partially due to the Hoffman's intelligent partnering with wineries through which the Hoffmans sold their books. The wineries mentioned in the book wanted copies to sell in their gift shops.

Bob had a background in marketing and established outstanding distribution relationships via non-traditional channels. (Remember, the motto of many small publishers is "Bookstores are the worst place to sell books!") Bob also focused upon a well-defined market niche, which he felt passionate about.

→ associated /integrated marketing / promotion.

Today, The Hoffman Press uses an order fulfillment company to pack and ship their books. That's probably a good thing, because The Hoffman Press sells over 100,000 cookbooks a year.

Planting Editorial Material

↳ Product Placement in your books,

Many publishers contemplate the marketing of a book *before* writing or acquiring it and then they publish a book that is inherently more marketable by carefully planting content. Sometimes, this is known as 'planting editorial material.'

As an example, suppose you write a book about home improvement. If you mention specific home-improvement companies, home-improvement products, home-improvement magazines, TV, radio shows, and related books by home-improvement writers, you enhance the possibilities of having your book favorably mentioned by those companies, magazines, and authors.

In fact, this 'planting of editorial material' relies upon another technique of influence called 'reciprocation.' If you do nice things for other people, they often feel obliged to do nice things for you. But, you must be careful. If it appears you're too manipulative, 'reciprocation' can backfire on you.

Another important caveat is that you must always think first of the reader of your books and provide them quality information. Never promote shoddy products in an attempt to promote your own book. If you do this, you run the serious risk of disappointing readers, because they are dissatisfied with a product you recommend. And, remember, people who are unhappy with a product or service often tell their friends to avoid the product.

But, by recommending high-quality, related products, etc., you not only provide a valuable resource to your readers, but you also *enhance the marketability of your books.*

Product placement isn't anything new. It's especially common in movies. One great example is the fun film *Castaway* starring Tom Hanks. If any film deserves an Academy Award for product placement, it's *Castaway*. For the first five minutes, I wasn't sure if I was watching a movie or a Fed Ex commercial. Then, Hanks's friend on the deserted island is a soccer ball, named *Wilson*. Hanks is rescued only to learn that his girlfriend has remarried. She thought he was dead and gave up hope.

In the end of the film, jilted in love, but still a devoted Fed-Ex employee, Hanks delivers the Fed-Ex package that kept him going on the deserted island until he was rescued (the thought of delivering it gave him hope and a reason to get off the island). He delivers it to a beautiful, single, and artistic women. Gosh, Fed Ex must be a great place to work for a young, energetic, and single person! Companies pay big money for that kind of publicity. Even if you can't count on love, you can count on Fed Ex.

Small publishers can learn to benefit from product placement. Don't expect to get paid money for mentioning products as movies do, but you might enhance distribution and publicity opportunities. As your company becomes more successful and your own influence grows, more and more people will help you and your authors because *you'll* be positioned to help them.

Online Book Marketing

The Internet has revolutionized book sales and continues to do so. In fact, several bestselling books started, not as books, but as popular websites. Consider the success of the Motley Fool, the investment website, which became the basis for the bestselling investment books based upon that name.

Many with popular websites find that even if they can't generate income in any other way, such as banner advertising, they can promote their own books and do quite well. Previously, we said that you should select your authors based upon their marketability. Sometimes, that marketability comes from an established following and sometimes that following comes from the Internet.

One new publisher who has benefited greatly from the Internet is computer book writer Peter Kent, who created the popular line of "Poor Richard's Books" (www.topfloor.com) which cover topics such as Internet marketing and establishing a cost-effective website.

Small publishers can either design and build their own websites or hire a designer to create a basic website. The basics of Hyper Text Mark Up Language (html), which is used to create basic web pages, is quite simple, and there are many computer programs designed to make web page design easy.

One possibility to design an inexpensive website is to ask your local community college if it has any graphic arts or web design students who'd like to design a low-cost site for you. Ask to see the student's portfolio of previous work.

Only a few years ago, someone could learn html in a weekend and earn $60,000 a year designing websites. The basic skills were that easy to learn and rare at the time. Today, nearly every graphic design student knows html and designers can be hired at very reasonable rates. And, e-commerce functions, such as secure online ordering, are being offered regularly from web hosting companies as part of their standard web hosting packages.

Some publishers have been very successful with Internet marketing. Building enough traffic to make web marketing very profitable isn't trivial. But, the profit margin offered by individual customer sales online is great.

Remember, most traditional distribution channels take 55% of the retail price of the book. Online marketing can offer the book for the full retail price, and you might only pay 2% of that for credit card processing. That can translate into a difference of three or even four times in profitability, depending upon the price of your books and other factors. It might take 100,000 bookstore sales to equal the profitability of 30,000 online sales.

Veltisezar Bautista, owner of Bookhaus Publishers (bookhaus.com) and author of *How to Build a Successful One-Person Business*, does volume sales through a distributor to bookstores, but he still sells more of his popular book, *The Book of U.S. Postal Exams: How to Score 95-100%*, online. Why do online sales dominate his distributor sales?

Velty says, "Because my sixteen websites are selling my books night and day, 24 hours a day, 7 days a week, 12 months a year. And I do an aggressive Internet promotion. (It's survival of the fittest on the Internet.)"

Affiliate Marketing

One unique area of online marketing is the potential for affiliate marketing. Most publishers are familiar with amazon.com's affiliate marketing program called Amazon Associates.

Basically, individual websites link to individual books at Amazon and if a potential book buyer follows the link and decides to buy the book from Amazon, the website owner is paid a commission of 5% to 15% of the book's price.

If you have a book promotional website, you might want to link your book's site to amazon.com because many people will hesitate to use a credit card over the Internet to purchase goods from your unknown company. But, they might purchase online through amazon.com.

The other opportunity for publishers is to *create affiliate marketing programs of their own*. One goal of websites is to generate links to your site from other websites. This 'link popularity' is used by many popular search engines to determine the ranking in the returned search results. Sites which have many inbound links tend to rank higher than sites with few links to them. Even search-engine automatons rely upon 'social proof'!

One day, while browsing the Internet, I came upon a link to an Internet marketing course. I haven't examined the course so I can't recommend it, nor am I being critical of it. Because I know nothing about its quality, I won't mention its website. But promoting the course made very effective use of affiliate marketing. In particular, for a $200 course, the affiliates received about a 30% commission if a sale resulted from the buyer following their link to the course. That's a commission of about $60 per sale.

I think we'll see more and more of this type of marketing in the future. Someone offers a relatively high-end course and gives affiliates a good $60 or so to generate as many affiliates as possible. Each of those affiliates creates an incoming link and creates the chance of making a sale. This particular course had about 10,000 links to it! And, the Internet promoter claims to earn millions of dollars promoting his course.

→ an income link :).

The issue I have with such a plan is that it seems many affiliates just link to the thing for the money and give it rave reviews without mentioning that they get a commission if you follow the link and buy the product. Many recommend the course without ever seeing it. That seems a bit disingenuous to me.

One problem with having an affiliate marketing program is that there is a real possibility of fraud against your program. Some people will create an affiliate link and generate many fraudulent sales in an attempt to generate inflated commissions. Again, there are standard defenses you can take to prevent such shenanigans. And, if you select your affiliates carefully, you reduce the risk of inviting problems of that nature.

If you have a product that supports adequate profit margins, affiliate marketing might prove effective for you. Otherwise, have people who want to link to your book online do so via amazon.com and the other established online booksellers.

Free Publicity And News Releases

One advantage to selling books is that books tend to generate much press relative to other products. Free publicity is always more effective than paid advertising. Paid advertising is expensive, and people distrust advertising. The key to getting free publicity is not to be too self-promotional. Serious media outlets will simply toss out any news release which is obviously just self-promotional.

But, if in addition to being *somewhat* self-promotional, your news release provides some news or entertainment value, there's a better chance your news release will be used by the media or you'll be featured in the media. Have your authors become valuable interview experts who provide solid information to the media.

There are many organizations that send out targeted news releases. One respected company serving the small press community is Paul Krupin's imediafax.com, which faxes targeted news releases for $0.25 per release per page. These news releases are only sent to reporters and media outlets that wish to receive them.

Thus, to reach 400 media sources costs about $100. Paul is also the author of *Trash-Proof News Releases: The Surefire Way To Get Publicity*, which can help you learn to write more effective press releases.

The most successful book promoters are masters at getting free publicity. By selling related books, you'll be able to reuse media contacts you've established. For each new topic you write about, you'll need to find new media contacts who cover the new area.

Another excellent source of publicity is public speaking. Many bestselling authors are public speakers. And, many authors generate substantial income through paid speaking engagements. To help get your authors media recognition, consider listing them with organizations, such as GuestFinder.com, which make public speakers available to the media.

Book Reviews

While there are many book reviewers and book review sources, only a few are truly receptive to small publisher titles. Jim Cox's *Midwest Book Review* (www.midwestbookreview.com) should definitely receive a review copy of your small press titles.

Books reviewed by MBR are included in Gale Research Group's *Book Review Index* on CD-ROM which is distributed to corporate, academic, and public library systems. MBR reviews often turn up on amazon.com and other places. In addition, MBR has several online book review magazines, which include *Small Press Bookwatch*, which is devoted exclusively to reviewing small press titles.

I believe MBR has been one of the most positive forces helping small press titles achieve recognition. I've always noticed a boost in sales when one of our HCM titles has been reviewed by MBR. MBR depends upon volunteer reviewers and receives a great many books, so don't feel bad if your title isn't chosen for review.

Jim Cox says: "Of the 1500+ titles a month received, about half (750) get assigned, and only around 450+ get reviewed. That's about 1/3 of the total submitted." However, that review percentage is probably far greater than any other source.

In addition, if you participate in the Amazon Advantage Program, you should send your titles to amazon.com for possible review (Amazon.com Books Editorial, P.O. Box 81226, Seattle, WA 98108-1226). Include a note saying that your books are small press titles.

While *Midwest Book Review* and many review sources are willing to review recently published books, some review sources will only consider reviewing 'prepublication' books. The American Library Association's *Booklist* (www.ala.org) is one prepublication reviewer. You must send prepublication reviewers copies *three months* in advance of your publication date.

You can have a POD printer produce a short run of 'galley' copies to send to prepublication reviewers. Personally, because many small publishers can publish a book in *under* three months and because many prepublication reviewers either aren't particularly receptive to independent press titles or are swamped with books (*Booklist* receives over 30,000 titles each year), I don't bother to send review copies to conventional prepublication review sources. I'd rather focus upon getting books to columnists and other people who write about the book's topic.

Getting Books Into Bookstores

While many small publishers have the motto, "Bookstores are the worst place to sell books," many publishers have gotten their small press titles onto the shelves of the big name bookstores. Often, these publishers depend upon bookstore sales for steady income.

Suzanne Thomas, author of the bestselling book, *Rental Houses for the Successful Small Investor*, has been very successful in getting her book into stores. She describes the process for getting books into Barnes and Noble stores:

> Model is the term Barnes & Noble uses, so I use it too. They 'model' a book to be carried by a store. When the book sells, the computer automatically reorders another copy. A store could be modeled to carry one or more copies per store, although not necessarily for all

stores (they do pay attention to what topics sell best in each region).

In contrast, if I get a manager to order a copy of one of my books just to try it, I need to check whether it sells. If it does, then I can ask the manager to order another copy. This method is far more time consuming than having a computer order automatically, but sometimes I have to use it to get a book selling. Once I prove a book will sell, then B&N might decide to model it for some stores.

Sometimes B&N will model a brand new book for some of their stores when a publisher submits it to the Small Press Dept. in New York. (122 Fifth Ave., NY, NY 10011)

I used booksignings very successfully with my first book, *Rental Houses for the Successful Small Investor*. I did 13 signings with B&N stores the first year it was out, and 6 the next year. Each signing sold 25-30 books over a month, or about 500 copies. Plus this book was also selling copies in the stores that were modeled to carry it (I intentionally tried to set up book signings in stores not modeled to carry this title). Two years later, instead of being modeled in approximately 50 stores, this book is modeled in almost all the B&N stores. Based on my knowledge of desired turnover in bookstores, I believe that as long as 4-6 copies sell per year per store, they'll keep automatically stocking it (modeling it) for these stores.

Many experienced publishers recommend a master (i.e., exclusive) distributor if you wish to get your books onto bookstore shelves. Master distributors don't just make your titles available to bookstores, they actively promote them. (We discuss the dangers of working with a master distributor in another chapter.) Plus, it's important to have a title that appeals to a general readership if you hope to see your books in bookstores.

Award-winning publisher Veltisezar Bautista (bookhaus.com), who publishes books about a wide range of topics explains:

> I think that there are two types of publishers (or self-publishers): those who love distributors and those who hate distributors.
>
> If your book/books sell to (or through) bookstores, you love distributors. If your books are geared toward a niche market, they may not sell through bookstores and you may not need a distributor. Also, if your books are not for the general public, bookstores may not accept them for placement on their shelves. Yes, it's plain and simple: there are books that are ideal for bookstore selling, and there are books that don't sell in bookstores.
>
> For example, my title, *The Book of U.S. Postal Exams: How to Score 95-100%* sells well in bookstores and on the Internet. It won the 1998 No. 1 Bestselling Title Award (in study guides) from Amazon.com.
>
> However, my book, *The Filipino Americans (1763-Present): Their History, Culture, and Traditions* is not sold in bookstores. Bookstore customers special order it. But it sells well to public and school libraries. In fact, it is used as a textbook in Asian Studies and Filipino American Studies at the San Diego State University and other colleges.
>
> Since 1985, my distributor, Publishers Group West (the largest of them all) has been sending me checks month after month, year after year. Imagine, I just send my books to them by truck. They keep the books in their warehouse, their representatives sell my books to wholesalers and bookstores, and they collect the payments. Then my distributor never forgets to send my monthly checks. It's like I'm receiving big pension checks every month! Yes, a one-person business owner (like me) needs a distributor.

Book Promotion And Turn Key Fulfillment

As Velty points out, if you want to run a one-person publishing company and also have a huge level of sales, you *need* to outsource fulfillment. You aren't going to pack and ship 100,000 books a year by yourself! You won't have any time left for marketing and writing! You probably won't want to pack and ship 10,000 books a year either!

You have two options: 1) Use a master distributor who promotes, stores, and ships your books; or 2) Hire a fulfillment agency which only stores and ships your books.

To help you choose between these options, contemplate how you'll market your books, whether bookstore sales are important to you, and whether or not you're willing to accept the risk of having an exclusive distributor.

Book Pricing And Book Industry Terms—How Not To Lose Your Shirt!

Setting Your Discount Schedule

Every once in a while I stumble upon a website promoting an unheard of POD printer or vanity press publisher. Vanity presses are different from usual publishers in that they charge their authors to produce the author's book. Conventional publishers don't charge authors to publish their books. Conventional publishers make their money by selling books to readers.

Typically, vanity publishers don't earn their money by selling books to readers. They make their money selling books to authors. Authors usually don't make money if they get involved with a vanity press publisher. In my opinion, authors become a source of profit to someone trying to exploit them when they use vanity publishers.

One argument I saw promoting a small printer went something like the following: "Assume your book is priced at $19.95. The cost to print the book with us is only $6. Thus, you have a profit per book of $13.95. If you print 500 books, you can earn an amazing $6,975 profit with only an investment of $3,000!"

Actually, the printer's cost of $6 a book was very high. And, most book sales do not net publishers anywhere near the full retail price of the book.

Books from small publishers are typically distributed in the following fashion: A person decides he or she wants to buy a book and orders it from the local bookstore. The person might have heard about the book on a radio show, TV show, or it was mentioned in a newspaper article. The bookstore, in turn, orders it directly from the publisher, or, more often, orders it from a distributor, such as Ingram. Assume the bookstore places the order with Ingram.

To get your book distributed by Ingram means that you'll receive a wholesale price of 45% of the retail price of the book. The standard industry 'trade discount' in the book publishing trade is 55%. This means that of every $1 in retail book price, $0.55 goes to the distributor and to the bookstore. Forty-five cents goes to you. That discount allows both the book distributor and the bookseller to earn a profit.

Working with the industry standard discount of 55%, for a single copy sale, priced at $19.95, you will receive $8.98. If the book costs $6 to produce, you only have a gross profit margin of $2.98 per book. And, that 'gross' profit must cover all of your other costs and expenses that are not included with the cost of producing the book.

Let's assume the book is ordered individually. Distributors do order 'onesies" as they're called by small publishers. If the book weighs under a pound and is shipped via the United States Post Office (USPS) at current postal rates, that will cost you $1.42. The bubble mailing folder to ship the book might cost $0.30. After these expenses, your profit per unit is $1.26. Further, you must invoice the distributor. That's $0.37 for the postage stamp.

After all these expenses, you have about $1. And, you're not done yet! You still have other overhead expenses to cover. What remains must be adequate compensation for your time in packing and shipping the book. Clearly, in this case, a "onesie," sold at the full wholesale discount isn't a profitable endeavor for a small publisher! You don't want to sell one book at a time and offer a 55% discount. It's just not worth it!

Wholesale discounts are based upon the premise that the wholesaler will order many copies at a time. Theoretically, wholesalers deal in bulk orders. Unfortunately, many larger distributors demand the full 55% discount even if they are only ordering a few copies at a time. This can be a bad situation for a small publisher.

One possibility is to reduce your production costs. Remember, printing is a competitive field. You should get quotes from many reliable printers before choosing a printer. Every penny saved in printing costs drops to the bottom line. If, rather than printing your copies at $6 per unit, you do a larger press run and get them produced for $3 per unit, that's $3 more per unit sale that *you'll* earn. In another chapter, I discuss the disadvantages of trying to push your per-unit-cost down by printing more copies.

While you must be frugal, you also want to assure adequate production quality. An inexpensive printing job is no bargain if the books are poorly produced. Especially for a new publisher, I'd suggest working with an established printer with an excellent reputation in the small press community.

Another option is to sell more books. If Ingram has much more demand for your book, rather than ordering one book, maybe, they'll order 100 at a time. Your postage cost per unit to send the books to Ingram will drop dramatically. The cost of things, such as a $0.37 stamp to send an invoice, will become trivial relative to the overall size of the order. Overall, then, you can make a reasonable profit.

The other option is to have a discount schedule that differs from a flat 55% discount at the wholesale level. A discount schedule tells wholesalers and retailers who want to order your book how much discount they receive based upon the number of copies ordered.

For example, a common discount schedule is the following:

1 copy ordered	No Discount
2-4 copies ordered	25% 'short' discount
5-19 copies ordered	40% discount
20 or more copies ordered	55% discount

If you adopt a discount schedule based upon the number of copies ordered, you'll probably want to base it *only* upon the number of books ordered. Some people try to create schedules based upon the number of copies ordered and the type of organization ordering the book. The theory is that 'distributors' should get a larger discount than a 'bookstore,' because 'distributors' tend to order more copies. This makes little sense! Your discount schedule is already based upon the number of copies ordered! Plus, everyone who orders a book will claim to be a 'wholesaler' or a 'distributor' to get your maximum discount.

While setting a discount schedule, such as the above, is generally a good idea, it's important to know that the largest bookstore distributor, Ingram, won't accept non-standard terms from a small publisher. This means they won't order your book. That means that bookstores won't be able to order it from them. Some bookstores will go out of their way to fill a customer's special order. Others won't.

One possibility would seem to be to allow Ingram the industry 55% discount, but disallow that discount to other distributors. Unfortunately, that pricing is illegal. You must offer equivalent terms to equivalent business types. In other words, if you allow Ingram a 55% discount, it's only fair to also give Baker & Taylor, another big distributor, and other distributors a 55% discount. If you offer a 40% discount to one bookstore, you should offer a 40% discount to all bookstores.

Many new publishers become confused by the requirement that you must offer similar companies similar discounts. This doesn't mean that you must sell to everyone on any terms. In particular, if you're dealing with a bookstore or a distributor unknown to you, there isn't any harm in demanding prepayment. You can and should only extend credit to companies you trust.

Prepayment Versus Credit

In most industries selling to customers on credit terms is standard. It's also standard in the book industry. However, there's an annoying aspect to credit sales in the book industry. Many small bookstores will order a single copy from a small publisher and not pay the small publisher.

What are you going to do to collect a $19.95 payment? You can call. You can cajole. You can threaten (if you do this, be sure you understand the legalities of collection techniques). But, effectively, that's about it. The amount is too small to allow any really effective collection techniques.

Now, don't get me wrong. I'm no pancake from being driven over in business deals. But, what can you do for $19.95? Any attempt to collect costs more than the amount collected, and small bookstores know this! And, many are unethical enough to try to benefit from it. So, effectively, if you extend credit to unknown bookstores, be prepared to write it off as a bad debt!

Many small publishers will only sell to individual bookstores on a prepay basis. I highly recommend adopting pre-pay terms. Or, refer the unknown bookstore to Ingram, Baker & Taylor, or another distributor who distributes your book. Remember, if you fill an order but don't receive payment, you're out the cost of producing the book, plus the cost of shipping the book.

Many people new to business underestimate the effect on profitability that bad debts have. Suppose you earn a net profit of $2 per book for every book sold and that your books cost $2 to produce. You accept credit terms, and a bookstore orders one copy of your book and doesn't pay. After allowing for packing and mailing costs, you've probably spent $4 total to ship them that book. This means the single non-pay 'sale' will require *two* profitable book sales to offset the costs of fulfilling that unpaid order.

Overall, when setting your discount schedule and credit terms, be sure to adopt policies that are sufficiently favorable to you to allow your publishing company to profit. I recommend pricing your books sufficiently high so that you can even allow a small profit on a single copy sale sold to a distributor at the full 55% trade discount. This means your books will be relatively high-priced. But, it's the only way to assure that you won't wind up filling orders that cost you money! Price your books too low, and you might lose money with every sale.

Book Pricing

Many books are marked up by a factor of three to ten times their unit production cost. Lower-priced books typically need to be 'marked up' more. However, when setting a book's price don't just use an arbitrary mark up. Always estimate your gross profit margin and use that as a guide to setting your book's price.

Take your estimated retail price and multiply it by 0.45. That's typically how much you'll collect. From that subtract the estimated per-unit printing cost of your book to get the gross profit margin per book measured in dollars. Be sure to include inbound freight from your printer in your book's per unit cost.

That gross profit must cover all other expenses and allow you to make a decent profit. If not, you must raise your price. There is a danger of setting your book's price too high. You don't want potential customers to avoid your book because they feel it's too expensive.

To be sure your title isn't too expensive, examine similar titles on amazon.com or elsewhere. Play with some possible retail prices to find a value that offers a decent profit while also allowing a reasonable retail price.

Some customers will feel your pricing is too high. But, I wouldn't worry about that. I'd rather lose a few sales than lose money! I recommend you provide high-quality information and aim to publish upper-priced books. Higher-priced specialty titles are often profitable. Consider this: If you earn $6 per book publishing a $34.95 business or technical book and only $2 publishing a $15.95 general title, the general title must sell three times as many copies for you to earn as much as you would earn selling your specialty title.

Many of the costs, such as cover design, are the same with either title. Other costs, such as editing and page layout expenses, aren't really that much more. Thus, your investment in launching a higher-end title isn't much more than launching a general title.

Assume you'd be happy to sell 100,000 copies of your general title. To earn an equivalent profit would only demand about 33,000 sales of a specialty title. And, a quality specialty title might offer strong sales for a decade or more.

If you're writing the books yourself, shorter books of lower price do offer the advantage of being easier to complete. That lets you get more titles out.

Incidentally, I've noticed that many small publishers who participate in Amazon's Advantage program sell thousands of books each year through amazon.com. Yet, Amazon doesn't discount their titles. Back when Amazon started, there was a competitive price war between Amazon, Barnes & Noble, and the other big bookstores. Many were discounting books by 20% or even 30%. Don't assume that the online bookstores will discount your book when you set its price. Assume your book will sell to the end customer for its stated retail price.

Returns And The Book Trade

Book returns are another annoying aspect of the book trade. If you're like most small publishers and you sell through non-traditional outlets, your returns won't be nearly as big a problem. Many small publishers say that bookstores are the worst place to sell books.

Typically, with large publishers and bookstores, the following happens: A publisher produces a book and spends a great deal of money on advertising. Because the booksellers know the book will be heavily promoted, they're willing to stock it in their bookstores in the hope that customers shopping in the store will buy a copy.

Of course, a book has a much better chance of selling if customers can find it on the shelves. Once a book is heavily promoted and commonly available at many bookstores, most other bookstores will want to stock it. This is a case of the strong getting stronger. It's also the reason that, if you publish other authors, you should be just as concerned with the marketability and celebrity level of the author. Will that author be a good book promoter? Is the person someone who can get media attention or who already has an established following? If not, the author could write the best book in the world and it might only sell fifty copies worldwide.

So, bookstores will order many copies from the distributor. The distributor will fill the orders by ordering, say, 20,000 copies from the publisher. The distributor will send the books to individual bookstores. Then, the books will go on the shelves. Some will sell.

But, some books will fall on the floor and have their covers bent. People don't like buying books with bent covers. Some patrons will examine the books with dirty hands and leave little smudge marks on the books. Some children will get sticky candy on the books. Some books will sit untouched and remain in pristine condition.

To make way for newer books, which are getting more promotion, the damaged and unselling copies will be returned to the distributor for a refund. The distributor, in turn, will return them to the publisher for a refund. Maybe 3,000 copies will be returned. Maybe 5,000 copies will be returned. The more aggressive the distributor and the publisher are in getting books on shelves, the higher the return rate will be. It's not uncommon to have ten percent of the books returned.

Many of those copies are damaged and must be written-off or sold at a discount (some publishers sell damaged copies as used books on Amazon). Even if the books were in great shape, there's a chance they weren't adequately packed for their return trip to you and they were damaged in transit.

In addition, the publisher has paid shipping charges to get the books to the distributor. To add insult to injury, many distributors will charge the publisher for return postage. This whole scheme works because so many books were produced that the cost per unit was very small. And, so many books are shipped at one time that the postage per book wasn't too bad either.

Now, consider the case of a small publisher. Your per-unit costs are higher. You don't have the mass media blitz. Nor do you usually have big-name celebrity authors, such as Bill Clinton, who received a $10 million advance for his book. Bookstore returns could easily do in a small publisher.

Book returns and non-payment from some exclusive distributors could also do in a small publisher. Non-exclusive distributors, sometimes called wholesalers, such as Ingram and Baker & Taylor, serve as order fillers only. They don't actively try to *sell* small publisher titles to bookstores. *And, you can make your titles available through all wholesalers.* Master distributors, who usually want exclusivity and who will try to 'sell' your book to the trade, i.e., bookstores, also exist. In dealing with exclusive distributors, you must exercise caution.

I've known many publishers of all sizes. Only a few have had a good relationship with a master distributor. Most small publishers will recommend avoiding master distributors.

I've heard of cases where a master distributor did a great job of placing books. Something like 10,000 books were requested. The publisher printed 10,000 copies. Several months later 9,000 copies were returned for a refund. Many of them damaged! Obviously, as a small publisher, you don't want that!

It's difficult to draw conclusions when many books go out and come back. If the books got on bookstore shelves, the distributor did a great job, and you really need 'pull advertising' to sell the books, better books, or something else. On the other hand, if the books were ordered and shipped, but never really displayed on bookstore shelves, the distributor didn't do a good job. If you place your books in bookstores through a master distributor, you might want to check some individual stores to see if your books are available.

When bookstores order single copies to fill special customer requests for a book, there tend to be few, if any, returns. Just as I recommend demanding prepayment from unknown bookstores, I recommend you consider having a no-returns policy when dealing with the trade. Offsetting this is the complication that Ingram also demands the ability to return books as part of its 'standard' terms.

It's important to note that a no-returns policy has nothing to do with the quality of your books. Your books should be so good that the vast majority of readers wouldn't want a refund. It has to do with the fundamental behavior of distribution within the book trade. I've known of cases where a distributor returned books and the same day ordered the exact same books from a publisher. And, often, the distributor expects immediate compensation for the returned books, while expecting to take the 'industry standard' payment terms of 90 days for the books just ordered! That's unacceptable to a small publisher.

If you allow returns, you might want to start tracking how much profitability is lost due to returns. Divide the cost of the returns by the number of books you profitably sold to estimate the expense per unit due to returns. Then, you can see how returns affect a title's profitability. If necessary, you can allow for the expense of returns by increasing the book's retail price.

As an example, assume that for every twenty books sold you get one return. Assume the returned book is damaged and not saleable. Assume the book's per unit cost is $3. Assume the return costs you $1 in return postage and $0.75 in other fulfillment (unfulfillment?) costs (maybe, your fulfillment company has a charge for processing returned books). The total expense of a returned book is $4.75.

Dividing that by nineteen gives $0.25 per book expense due to returns. That's how much the profitability of every unit sold is reduced.

Some publishers explicitly factor returns into their book's pricing. But, I think that's a bit extreme. Rather, just price your books sufficiently high so that you have plenty of gross profit margin per book and that will easily cover the added expense of returns!

90 Days To Payment—Cash Flow Problems In The Book Trade

When extending credit, it's expected the bill will be paid within a certain time period. Thirty days after receiving an invoice is the standard in many industries. For some odd reason, the 'industry standard' in the book publishing business is 90 days. This means that if you sell a book today, you need to wait about three months before you can expect to be paid.

That's why the compounding example in the chapter about Just-In-Time Inventory broke the year into quarterly periods. One dollar 'invested' in inventory can be 'recycled' four times in a year, if we assume the 'industry standard' three-month pay period.

Business Ratios

In many industries there are crucial business ratios which are used to evaluate the efficiency and health of a business. I don't want you to sweat business ratios if you're new to publishing. Many successful publishers never evaluate performance ratios. But, I want you to know they exist and be aware of the key things they're trying to measure.

Inventory Turnover

One important ratio is inventory turnover. Inventory turnover is a measure of how fast your products are selling. Higher inventory turnover usually means less risk for a business, because there isn't as much danger of winding up with highly-valued but unsellable inventory which must eventually be written-off.

Inventory turnover is measured as the cost of goods sold throughout the year divided by the average inventory in stock over the year. You can calculate inventory turnover for all your inventory collectively. But, I'd recommend calculating it for each title individually. (Or, you can ignore the calculations altogether. Just remember that you want your books to be selling. You don't want to have thousands of copies sitting around for years.)

Cost of goods sold is just what you might think it is. It's the cost of your books sold. So, assume you printed 1,000 copies at the start of the year and they cost you $3,000. At the end of the year, you've sold all of your inventory.

The average value of your inventory is 1/2($3,000 + 0) = $1,500. Notice that you have no inventory at the end of the year, so your average inventory is just half your starting inventory.

The cost of goods sold in this case is $3,000 because you've sold all of your books. So, the inventory turnover is two. This means your average level of inventory sells out in six months.

Now, if at the end of the year, you've only sold 200 books, the cost of goods sold is $600. (There are two ways to figure cost-of-goods-sold, and they're essentially the same calculation. One is to calculate your per-unit cost for the books based upon their initial production costs and then multiply that times the number of books sold throughout the year. In this case, the average cost per book is $3,000/1,000 or $3. And, 200 books sold have a cost of $600. The other way to calculate cost-of-goods-sold is to use the same procedure as you would for your income tax returns. Calculate the starting inventory minus the ending inventory—assuming no additions to inventory or revaluation adjustments, which we discuss in another chapter. In that case, the ending inventory is 800 copies. If we multiply $3,000 by the ratio of 800/1,000 we see that the ending value of inventory is $2,400 because the percentage of inventory remaining is 800/1,000. That's also the percentage of initial 'investment' remaining. Subtracting $2,400 from $3,000 gives $600 as the cost of goods sold.)

So, if we sold 200 copies, our average inventory count is (1,000 + 800)/2 = 900 copies, which represents $2,700 in value. Thus, our inventory turnover is (cost-of-goods-sold)/(average inventory) = $600/$2,700 = 0.22. An inventory turnover ratio of less than one means that it takes over a year to sell your average inventory. If you invert 0.22 by dividing it into one, you get 4.5. That represents the number of years it will take to sell your average inventory. (You can double check this as follows: Your average inventory has a value of $2,700, which represents 900 copies. If you continue to sell 200 copies a year, it will take 4.5 years to sell all 900 copies.)

Having an inventory turnover of two or three years isn't a problem, if you have storage room for the titles and if you're saving a good deal of money on your per-unit production costs for the book by printing the book in larger press runs. But, if you have other titles you want to publish and your company is cash strapped, you might want to shorten the amount of time your inventory sits by increasing your inventory turnover.

Hopefully, your book will take off and start to sell far more than 200 copies a year! You want to track how much inventory you have on hand relative to how fast your book is selling. Be sure to reprint your titles when you still have about a two-month supply of inventory.

So, for example, if your book consistently sells 6,000 copies a year, that's a sales rate of 500 per month. You'd want to reprint when you had 1,000 copies in stock. A two-month lead time helps assure you won't run out of inventory.

Keeping Track Of Accounts Receivable

Publishers will also want to monitor accounts receivable. Accounts receivable is money owed to you by other companies. Rather than calculating one single ratio to monitor your collection performance, you should create an aging schedule for each account, if necessary. For every vendor who buys your books, make a list of all unpaid orders. Add up the amounts to see how much you're owed and how current the other company is in paying you. An aging schedule looks something like this:

Current (payment not due yet)	$1,398	56%
1 day to 30 days overdue	300	12%
31 days to 60 days overdue	499	20%
61 days to 90 days overdue	300	12%
More than 90 days overdue	0	0%
	$2,497	100%

The numbers in the second column represent how much money is owed. We see the distributor owes us a total of $2,497. Of this $1,398 isn't due yet; $300 is overdue one to 30 days; $499 is overdue more than 30 days, but less than 60 days, etc.

The last column represents the percentage of the total account that is in each aging period. Notice the distributor is doing OK, but that 44% of the accounts are overdue.

We should also look at the history of payments from the distributor. If the total paid by the distributor in the last year greatly exceeds all the overdue accounts, you're probably OK. If the distributor has a history of no-pays, it will show up in the aging schedule.

Incidentally, if you grow as a business to the point where your company is a viable candidate for bank loans, the bank will look at an aging schedule to determine the collateral value of your accounts receivable. If you have $400,000 in accounts receivable and the great majority of it is current, that has much more collateral value than if you have $400,000 in accounts receivable and it's all more than 90 days overdue!

The longer a bill goes unpaid, the less chance you'll collect payment. This is why banks value current accounts more highly than overdue accounts.

Bankruptcy Of Distributors

Most of the bigger distributors are relatively good about paying regularly, but you need to be careful. Selling books and distributing books is a difficult industry. Many mid-sized distributors go bankrupt leaving small publishers with thousands of dollars in unpaid bills.

In the event of a distributor bankruptcy, it's possible you'll recover very little of what you're owed. And, that has hurt many small publishers. But, with the established distributors, such as Ingram, don't worry too much about not being paid. You'll probably collect payment in full. With smaller distributors, you'll want to be careful not to extend too much credit.

There's a saying that "The Squeaky Wheel Gets Oiled," which means that companies that consistently squeak about accounts overdue are more likely to get paid compared to companies that have accounts overdue, but don't enthusiastically follow up with letters and phone calls.

With the book industry, the entire industry squeaks. That's probably because it's a very old industry. Squeaking won't necessarily get you paid right away, but it will allow you the opportunity to inform the owing party that they really should pay you, because if they don't, you'll be unable to extend future credit to them. Let them know that's part of your policy. You have nothing against them, but when accounts hit a certain overdue level, you don't extend more credit. All future orders will need to be on a prepay basis.

From the distributor's standpoint, this is a more serious problem than a squeak. If the distributor can't get access to your books, he can't sell them to his customers. And, his customers might start to assume that publishers aren't willing to extend credit to him and that the distributor is in financial difficulty. So, distributors will often prepay those who demand it, even if they aren't able to pay all overdue accounts.

The above advice can save you thousands of dollars in the event of a distributor bankruptcy. Often, some overdue accounts will only receive pennies on the dollar when a company goes bankrupt. But, by monitoring accounts receivable and knowing when to demand prepayment, you might save yourself thousands of dollars through orders that are placed between the time that the distributor stops being able to pay overdue accounts and the time the distributor goes bankrupt or is reorganized.

It's also important to note that bankruptcy laws are designed to favor the bankrupt company. The idea of bankruptcy is that the courts prevent creditors from choking off a struggling company and preventing its operations. Formally, at this point, everything will be determined by the bankruptcy court. Depending upon the bankruptcy, either the company will reorganize and continue to exist in some form or else the company will be liquidated.

If you're owed money by a bankrupt company, you'll receive letters from the bankruptcy attorney and courts explaining everything to you. You usually don't need to appear in court, unless you want.

There is a rule of bankruptcy that says you can't change your business relationship with a company based only upon its filing for bankruptcy. In fact, companies are usually required by law to continue to supply a bankrupt company on the same terms and conditions that were in force before the company filed for bankruptcy.

This is why it's so important to monitor accounts receivable and move companies which are getting into trouble onto a prepay basis as part of a standard policy. If this isn't part of your policy, you might find that you're required by law to continue to feed books to a company in bankruptcy. That can be a problem for a struggling publisher. Sometimes, another company which is considering buying the company in bankruptcy will agree to pay all new bills of the company during the bankruptcy organization and you'll be paid regularly as the company is in bankruptcy. Other times, the inventory and other assets of the bankrupt company will be sold and the bankrupt company simply ceases to exist.

There is one other unique aspect of bankruptcy law. Payments made by a company right before the company goes bankrupt might be deemed to be inappropriate or 'preferential payments.' If so, the bankruptcy court might demand that the payment be reversed so the money goes back into the pool of resources available to creditors.

This is done to protect creditors. Suppose, for example, the CEO of a struggling company which is about to go bankrupt has loaned the company $50,000. Then, right before the company goes bankrupt, the CEO has the company repay the personal loan. Now, obviously, that's not fair if other creditors will only eventually receive pennies on the dollar!

So, the bankruptcy court might deem the CEO's loan repayment was a 'preferential payment' and demand that the CEO give back the

$50,000 to the company so that it can be distributed by the bankruptcy court.

There is a rare chance that a bankruptcy court might challenge a large payment made to a publishing company by a bankrupt distributor. However, if you can show that it's your standard operating policy to demand prepayment and cut off credit if overdue accounts aren't repaid in full, then the repayment was made in the ordinary course of business and isn't a 'preferential payment.' The payment had nothing to do with anticipation of the company's bankruptcy, because it's a policy applied to all distributors who fall significantly behind in payments.

Vigilance in collection is your friend! The most important aspect of accounts receivable is to follow a set routine. Bill customers as soon as possible after delivering your service or product. And, follow up promptly on delinquent accounts. Studies have shown that the longer you wait to collect a delinquent account, the less likely you are to collect the account ever.

Consignment Sales And Perfecting A Security Interest

Here's another hint from experienced publisher Rod Colvin, owner of Addicus Books (www.AddicusBooks.com): In addition to protecting your accounts receivable and contemplating what happens to money owed you, contemplate what happens to your books held by your distributor in the event of a distributor bankruptcy.

You don't want the distributor to sell *your* books to pay *other organizations'* accounts receivable, leaving *you* with a large, unpaid bill! It's conceivable your books could all be sold, but *you* wouldn't be paid for them! The distributor could default on the money you are owed.

As in many things in life, during a bankruptcy, there's a pecking order. There are 'secured creditors' and 'unsecured creditors.' Secured creditors are paid first. Then, if any money is left, unsecured creditors are paid. Usually, unsecured creditors don't receive much, if anything.

You want to be sure to establish that the books your distributor holds in inventory are *your* property. If the relationship between you and your distributor is a consignment relationship, you want to have that clearly established. Establish the proper documentation and keep your contracts.

Consignment means that the possession of the books is transferred to the distributor, but the books remain the publisher's property until the books are actually sold. The publisher is the consignor. The distributor is the consignee.

The old saying, "Possession is nine-tenths of the law" is wrong. *Paper* is nine-tenths of the law! In the contract between you and the distributor, be sure the relationship is outlined as a consignment relationship. That's the first step in 'perfecting a security interest' in your inventory, which is a fancy way of saying that you're proving the books belong to you.

After establishing a formal consignment relationship, you must comply with the Uniform Commercial Code (UCC) requirements for perfecting your security interest in the inventory. If you fail to do this, it's conceivable that your books could be sold, but the proceeds could go to other people and you'll be labeled an unsecured creditor who receives nothing.

The next step in showing that you're the owner of the books is filing a UCC-1 Financing Statement with each Secretary of State or filing office for *each state* in which the consignee does business. (I know. This sounds like it really sucks. But, just wait, it gets worse!) At the very least, file the statement in your state and the distributor's state of residence. Theoretically, you really *should* file in *every* state.

Next, to perfect your security interest, theoretically, the consignor must give written notice to all pre-existing secured creditors who have liens on inventory. If it's well-known that the distributor works on a consignment basis, this step might not be essential. So, documenting the nature of the distributor's business is valuable. For example, if the distributor's website says they operate on a consignment basis, save that web page.

These steps of perfecting your security interest in your inventory should occur before your inventory is shipped to the distributor. If your financial exposure is sufficiently great, you might want to contact an experienced business attorney to help you establish your security interest in your books.

When you're just starting, you probably don't need to worry about distributor bankruptcy—especially, if you don't use a master distributor. But, as your business grows, or if you have an exclusive distributor who holds many of your books, being aware of this issue could potentially save you hundreds of thousands of dollars in the event of a distributor bankruptcy.

When Rod's distributor of three years went bankrupt, his business savvy and alertness allowed him to safely recover his inventory. Addicus Books (www.AddicusBooks.com) had 40 titles in print at the time and the inventory was nearly 40,000 books.

Rod's advice to publishers:

> I am one of those publishers who loves HAVING a distributor. If you want books in bookstores, it's more expedient to have a distributor. If you're the type of publisher who wants to grow a particular line of books you must have distributorship.
>
> Our books (consumer health books) sell well in bookstores.... so we want them in those stores. However, we now have some 35,000 books in our distributor's warehouse. The days of keeping books in my garage and ME packing and shipping them (and I did that for the first years) are long gone. I couldn't do that if I wanted.
>
> And, I can report from experience that if...I rented warehouse space, hired people to pack and ship books, and hired a clerk to send/process invoices....I would pay much more than I currently pay a distributor.
>
> I, too, used to resist paying those seemingly high percentages a distributor took, but it's far cheaper to hire a distributor (for 25% of net) than to hire employees to do the work. PLUS....my distributor only gives the major chains a 50% percent discount (rather than 55%)...so I automatically save 5% in the deal right there.
>
> Bottom line: my opinion is that some of us need a distributor to get books into bookstores. That said, let me also say that, as a small publisher, I work daily to

find other markets to make us less dependent on the bookstores. As Dan Poynter used to say.....the bookstore game can be a dangerous one for small publishers (given returns etc.)

We publishers need to be very vigilant (I think) when we sign up with a distributor. Keep your ears and eyes open. I have found using a distributor (esp. since we have 40 titles) was a tremendous help. Clearly...they sold more books than I ever could have. And, they took the shipping, warehouse, billing, fulfillment out of our hands and gave us time for other things. AND, it is cost effective. Yes, that large discount stings..... BUT I don't think a business can hire people to do all those functions for anywhere near the price.

Finally....my advice for any publisher looking at any distributor...do your home work: research the company, visit them in person (and listen to your gut feelings), interview other publishers who use them. Also, file a UCC-1 paper with the Secretary of State in their state.....it is just a small piece of paper that says YOU own the stock...not the distributor.

Incidentally, Dan Poynter, author of *The Self-Publishing Manual: How to Write, Print and Sell Your Own Book,* was one of the early pioneers in self-publishing. His website is ParaPublishing.com.

Collection Ratio

Many businesses calculate some version of a collection ratio. That's a rough measure of how long on average it takes to convert accounts receivable into cash. Roughly, it's a measure of the average collection period for a company. If you don't want to mess with this ratio, don't worry about it. But, it's one more measure of performance you might want to know. There are several variations of this ratio.

If you're interested in comparing your ratios to others in the same industry, you can find average key business ratios in publications such *as Industry Norms and Key Business Ratios* (Dunn & Bradstreet) and *Annual Statement Studies* (Robert Morris) to see what other companies maintain. Your library should have one or the other.

Most commonly, the collection ratio is measured as follows:

$$\text{Collection Ratio} = \frac{\text{(Accounts Receivable)}}{\text{(Average Daily Sales For The Period)}}$$

Often, the value of accounts receivable is just taken as its value at the start of an accounting period—be it a month, a quarter, or a year. Sometimes, rather than using the value of accounts receivable at a given point in time, the average value of the accounts receivable over the period is used. In other words, add the value of accounts receivable at the start of the accounting period to the value of accounts receivable at the end of the accounting period and then divide the result by two to get the average.

Usually, noncredit, cash sales aren't included in the average daily sales for the period. But, for some purposes, such as evaluating possible cash-flow or compounding cycles for a company, they are. I discuss cash-flow cycles in more detail in my book, *Thinking Like An Entrepreneur: How To Make Intelligent Business Decisions That Will Lead To Success In Building And Growing Your Own Company.*

Calculate average daily sales by adding up all sales over the accounting period and dividing the result by the number of days in the accounting period. For example, if you have $150,000 in sales over one year, the average daily sales are about $411.

Assume the value of your accounts receivable at the start of the year is $5,000 and, at the end of the year, it's $15,000. The average accounts receivable over the year is $10,000.

Thus, the collection ratio is $10,000/($411 per day) = 24.3 days. This says that it takes about 24 days to convert accounts receivable into cash. Thus, the average collection period is approximately 24 days.

We can work backward to solidify our understanding of collection ratios. We've said it takes about 24 days to convert accounts receivable into cash. If you're a bit unsure of how we got the number or exactly what it means, we can notice that if we assume the average collection period is 24 days, that there are about 15 collection periods in a year. We see this by dividing 365 days per year by 24 days in a collection period to get fifteen collection periods.

Then, if we multiply our average accounts receivable of $10,000 by fifteen—which is equivalent to collecting our average accounts receivable fifteen times in a year—we get $150,000 which agrees with the value of our annual sales.

Finally, some people calculate accounts receivable turnover directly, which is just total credit sales divided by accounts receivable. We see that we get $150,000 divided by $10,000 or fifteen. This agrees with how we calculated it the other way.

Again, I want to emphasize that you don't need to worry about business ratios, such as inventory turnover and collection ratios, if you don't want to. Many successful small publishers do fine without ever doing such analysis. But, I want you to know these ratios exist in case you find them useful as a measure of your company's performance.

If your company grows or if you consider buying or investing in a small publishing company, these ratios become powerful because they help you see how a business is doing.

Success Can Kill You

It's the typical story plot. A hero has a burning desire for something. The hero struggles and sacrifices and sacrifices and struggles. But, eventually, he gets what he wants! And, it destroys him.

What many new self-publishers want is a bestseller. Something like *Who Moved My Cheese?* which has sold over 10 million copies worldwide. Even at a measly author's royalty of 10% of the retail cost of the book, we see the author has earned about $20 million.

The problem is that it's difficult for a small publisher to fill ten million sales, or even one million sales, in a short period of time. This is one reason many people who self-publish often sell a wildly successful book to a larger publisher.

Either publishing becomes too much work and they don't really want to build a larger company or else they lack the financial resources to push the book to all it can be. They lack the financial resources to print enough books to meet market demand.

As discussed, with a profitable book, you can bootstrap the book's sales. Even if you only have enough cash to print 1,000 copies at the start of the year, by keeping your inventory turnover high and reinvesting earnings, you can sell far more than 1,000 books in a year.

However, sometimes you can't meet market demand. Suppose you can only afford to print 5,000 copies, and they sell out immediately. Your distributors owe you quite a lot of money. But, it will be several months before you receive payment. And, you still have orders coming in.

You've done a great job selling your book. An incredible job. But, you don't have any books left to fill the new orders, and you've run out of money to produce more books. Even though you'll make a great profit on the books you've already sold, not receiving this money for months is a real problem, because you need that money to reinvest in more company growth, i.e., printing more books.

This is the cash-flow problem of a growing company. Many companies that have exceptional growth struggle with cash-flow. You're not paid immediately for your products, so you have trouble reinvesting money to create and supply more products. You should ask yourself the question: What will I do if my sales are so large that I can't supply the demand?

As mentioned, one possibility is to sell your book to a larger publisher. Be sure you get a great advance. Your book is selling, and it isn't just a test at this point.

Another possibility is to borrow money to print more copies and keep publishing the book yourself. If you borrow money, be sure you don't overextend yourself. Remember the problem of returns. You want to be sure you're controlling your financial exposure and not letting the risk get out of control. Controlled company growth is often better in the long run than explosive, cash-strapped growth that leads to serious business problems and glitches and, sometimes, company failure.

Of eBooks And Cash Flow

While you can only fill a fixed number of physical book sales in a period of time due to cash-flow issues and the need to reinvest cash to produce more books, eBooks are an example of a product with an infinitely short compounding or cash-flow cycle. It costs almost nothing to produce and distribute a new eBook. So, theoretically, you could sell 10 million eBooks in a year while still running your publishing company from your home while dressed in your bathrobe.

However, many people won't buy eBooks, and I don't know of any eBooks that have become bestsellers comparable to print book bestsellers. So, moving a bestselling book to an eBook is only one way to try to improve the cash flow of a bestselling title. The eBook will generate cash inflow without requiring cash outflow.

Some eBooks have done well for their authors and publishers. The most successful case I'm aware of is Angela Adair-Hoy of booklocker.com. Angela Adair-Hoy is one of the featured publishers in *Make Money Self-Publishing*: *Learn How from Fourteen Successful Small Publishers* by Suzanne P. Thomas.

Thomas tells us that Adair-Hoy's eBook on producing and selling eBooks earns her $5,000 per month. Her books were originally distributed by a company, booklocker.com, owned by another businessperson. But, Adair-Hoy's books were so successful she bought the company. Now Adair-Hoy distributes other authors via booklocker.com.

Business Structure

Business structure refers to the legal form of your publishing company. Your publishing company can be a sole proprietorship, a limited liability company, a partnership, or a corporation. If you form a corporation, you can have it taxed either as a regular C-corporation or as an S-corporation.

These structural business decisions aren't unique to self-publishing, and I've written extensively about this topic on my small business website, thinkinglike.com (under "articles about small business." Also see the link to my answers to business questions on ideacafe.com). I won't go into too much detail here. I'll only touch upon the most important points related directly to publishing companies.

If you form no other business structure, your company is, by default, a sole proprietorship. Partnerships are generally to be *avoided* because each partner becomes personally responsible for the debts of the company, including debts incurred by your business partner.

So, as an extreme case, suppose your business partner spends $1 million dollars to buy his brother-in-law's collection of essays about living in a trailer park. Then, he mysteriously disappears, leaving your company owing your bank $1 million. Your personal assets are fair game for the people who will try to collect payment for that debt. You are responsible for the liabilities of your partnership! If you want to know more about liability issues and business structure, I recommend my book, *Thinking Like An Entrepreneur.*

I'm not an attorney and not rendering legal advice. What follows is my own personal understanding of business structure and how it relates to publishing. *You should consult an experienced business attorney if you have questions about liability and business structure issues.*

If you start a business with anyone other than your spouse, I recommend you look into forming a corporation or a limited liability company. If you hire employees other than family members, I recommend either a corporation or a limited liability company. If you publish other authors, I suggest you form a corporation or a limited liability company. If you only self-publish your own work, you can remain a sole proprietorship, or if you want, you can become a corporation or a limited liability company.

Having business partners, employees, and publishing other authors poses a danger that your company might incur liabilities far beyond your control. *These liabilities could be incurred by the actions of other people associated with your company. But, ultimately, your company would be the one responsible to pay these liabilities.*

As a partnership or a sole proprietor, you and your company are considered *inseparable*. Any money your company owes, you also personally owe.

Suppose your new employee is negligent and tosses a book from your fifth floor office building toward the postman's bag, just as the postman checks the mailbox on the street corner below. You can't actually just drop books in the mail, but your employee doesn't know this yet. (Larger packages must be *hand delivered* to the USPS. This is a security measure so that people don't leave bombs or other dangerous devices at anyone's doorstep expecting the USPS to pick them up.) Rather than landing in the postman's bag, it hits him on the head. Unfortunately, the book's a hardcover, and it kills him. His family sues your company for damages.

Your company is responsible for the actions of its employees. You might find that you owe the postman's family several million dollars. If you've already built a successful publishing company and are personally worth several million dollars, your personal assets as well as your business assets are available to cover your company's liability. Unless you were somehow personally responsible for the accident, if you were incorporated, and if you've run your corporation as a corporation, it's unlikely that your personal assets would be at risk. Your corporation might be forced into bankruptcy, but you probably wouldn't be forced into personal bankruptcy.

You've seen how business partners and employees can misbehave and cost your company. The same is true of authors you publish. Again, you'll probably be careful to protect yourself through contracts and through carefully reading the work to be published. You'll nix anything that could generate a viable lawsuit. But, let's assume that something gets by your careful eye.

On Line 36, Page 102, your author slanders someone. That someone sues your company. Again, as the publisher, you'll have to defend this suit, settle it, or take some other action. But, personally, as the company founder, your personal assets are probably not at risk if you've incorporated. You're not personally responsible for the company's debts. So, even if your company is driven into bankruptcy, your personal assets are intact.

In this way, you should view corporate structure or limited liability business structure as a personal shield. But, what if you're only self-publishing your own books and you're sued? Typically, you'll be sued as *both the publisher and the author*. So, in this case, corporate structure wouldn't mean much. You and your company would largely suffer the same fate. This is why I personally feel that a self-publisher can operate as a sole proprietor. However, there's no harm in incorporating. In some instances, it might be beneficial.

There are a few tax benefits to incorporating and operating as either an S-corporation or a C-corporation. See *Thinking Like An Entrepreneur* for more information.

Sole Proprietorship—Schedule C, Schedule SE, and Estimated Tax Payments

If you don't form any other business structure, you are, by default, a sole proprietorship. This means you and your business are one and the same. When tax time rolls around, in addition to filing your personal tax return, you'll file Schedule C and report your business activities along with your regular 1040 tax return.

You'll probably also need to file Schedule SE, which is a computation of your self-employment tax (See IRS Publication 533, Self-Employment Tax). When you work for other people, Social

Security taxes are taken from your paycheck, and your employer also pays Social Security for you. When you're self employed (e.g., a sole proprietorship), you're expected to pay your own Social Security tax. This takes about 15% of your net income. Schedule SE shows you how to calculate your self-employment tax.

You'll also need to familiarize yourself with Form 1040-ES and quarterly estimated taxes (See IRS Publication 505, Tax Withholding And Estimated Taxes). Suppose you earn $30,000 during your first year of self-publishing. You're happy, and you should be. That's very good for your first year! But, you owe taxes on this income. The U.S. tax system is a 'pay-as-you-go' tax system.

You can't just wait until the end of the year and pay your taxes then. The IRS wants its money as you earn it. The reason for this is the time value of money. Money held now is worth more than money received later because it can be invested to earn more money. So, the IRS expects you to estimate your annual tax liability and pay in quarterly installments.

You'll probably want to go to the IRS website and look under business 'Forms and Publications' and get Publication 334 which will help you understand business taxes. All IRS Publications are free either as paper booklets or as Adobe Acrobat files. I also suggest getting a copy of *Small Time Operator* by Bernard Kamoroff.

All the forms, schedules, and publications might seem overwhelming at first. But, you'll quickly become familiar with small business tax reporting. Once you've been through the process, it will become very easy for you.

DBA

DBA stands for "Doing Business As," also known as a certificate of assumed name. Essentially, it's a way of letting people know who the individual is behind a company name. DBA is filed locally.

My understanding is that if you do business under your own full legal name, you do not need to file a certificate of assumed name. But, if you do business under *any other name*, such as "Big Man Books," then, you'll need to file a DBA.

There usually is a small fee to file a certificate of assumed name (under $100). Then, usually, you run a notice of the association between you and your assumed name in a qualified newspaper. The idea of newspaper publication is that people have the right to know who they are doing business with (Either that or newspapers have good state lobbyists!). This is somewhat archaic, because if your company is not doing business locally, for example, no customer will ever see it! But, take out the newspaper ad, anyway! It's considered necessary to complete the registration process in many states.

Your Secretary of State, or equivalent office, can get you the forms you need to register a name and the details of what else you must do. I like having a name you're doing business under registered for another reason. If someone else later comes along and starts using the exact same name, in my non-legal-eagle-beagle view, it's a form of documentation that you were already using the name. Of course, to protect your name nationally, you might want to trademark your name at www.uspto.gov. That costs about $325 at present.

Corporations and companies can also file assumed name certificates. If the company does business under any name other than the company's full legal name, a certificate of assumed name should be filed. And, the filing procedure is the same.

Assumed name certificates can also be filed to let people know your publishing company does business under an 'imprint' name. Imprints are essentially different identities you want associated with groups of your titles.

Suppose you publish cookbooks and you've named your company, "Ann's Good Cookbooks." Then, you start publishing children's books. Since we wouldn't expect "Ann's Good Cookbooks" publishes children's books, you might want to start an imprint. Maybe, "Ann's Good Children's Books."

Random House, Inc., for example, has many imprints, including Ballantine Books, Sierra Club Books, Alfred A. Knopf, and Bantam Books For Young Readers.

Many publishers recommend that a person not use his or her own name as the name of their publishing company because the company will look smaller and some people are more dubious of the quality of self-published books. Choose a quality name. Always think about the impression your name generates.

S-Corporations

How you run your business on a day-to-day basis isn't dependent upon whether you're a sole proprietor or a corporation. Those are only business registration issues that effect taxation, liability, and other interactions with the government. Which business structure you use determines the forms you must file with the government.

Many small businesses incorporate and become S-corporations. 'S' stands for Subchapter S of the IRS code, but it might as well stand for "small." S-corporations offer the liability protection of incorporation with some added tax benefits for small business owners.

For example, if your S-corporation earns profits, but that money isn't paid out as wages to you, the money isn't subject to employment tax. When you're growing a company, issues like that are important. Similarly, once you pay yourself a "reasonable" wage, you can pay the rest to yourself as S-corporation dividends which are only taxed once as personal income. Again, I refer you to my website, thinkinglike.com and my book, *Thinking Like An Entrepreneur*.

Reporting Author Royalties

If you publish other authors and pay them royalties, you'll need to become familiar with IRS Form 1099-MISC. Form 1099's are designed to let the IRS know about money paid to individuals that isn't subject to employment tax withholding. It's an informational form. You don't need to send the IRS any money. The form helps assure the IRS that authors are reporting their book royalties and paying income taxes on them.

You send copies of 1099-MISC to both your authors and to the IRS. The IRS also provides Form W-9, which is a form for requesting someone's Social Security number. W-9 is filled out by the author and returned to you. You don't file it with the IRS.

If you publish other authors, they might ask you whether book royalties should be reported on Schedule C as self-employment income, or, on Schedule E as 'Royalties.' The best answer is, "Consult your accountant or tax professional." The next best answer is probably "Schedule C."

If you're legally considered 'self-employed,' you *must* report royalties on Schedule C.

If you're not legally considered 'self-employed,' you *might* be able to report royalties on Schedule E. I like Schedule E! I don't like Schedule C. Earnings reported on Schedule C are not just income, but self-employment income, subject to self-employment tax at the rate of 15.3%.

According to my understanding of this, if you were a struggling writer, scrapping out a living and earning $15,000 from your writing, using Schedule C, you'd pay $2,295 in Social Security tax. You'd also get to deduct half of this tax from your personal income. So, if you're in the 28% tax bracket, because you have other earnings, you'd get to reduce your taxes by $321. Thus, you'd pay $1,973 in extra taxes.

But, if you were a politician with a cushy government job and you wrote a book and earned $60,000 in royalties, you *might* be able to report your royalties on Schedule E and pay no Social Security tax at all!

The lesson is that, as your company grows, spending a bit of time learning about taxes and various business structures might save you some significant money in taxes. When Thomas Stanley, bestselling coauthor of *The Millionaire Next Door: The Surprising Secrets of America's Wealthy*, surveyed the wealthy to determine the activity they engaged in the most, what would you guess they answered? Skiing in the Alps? Swimming in the Bahamas? Nope. Consulting with their tax advisor.

As a self-published author, you could pay yourself a royalty for each book sold. However, you don't need to do so, and I see little advantage in doing so. After generating sales and paying your expenses, whatever remains is your money, regardless of whether it's called business profit, royalties, or some combination of the two.

Sales Tax Questions And Use Tax Questions

Sales Tax

In most states, if you make retail book sales in your state, you'll need to collect state sales tax. Each state has very different laws about sales tax. Your state government is your best source of information for learning about state sales tax issues. Take advantage of the free information provided by your state government to learn about your state's sales tax! Many states offer free classes to help you understand the sales tax process. Remember, if you don't follow your state's laws, *you'll* be the one in trouble!

You'll generally need to apply for a state tax ID number, or a reseller's permit number, a seller's permit number, or your state will call it something else entirely. It basically amounts to a unique number to identify your company and acknowledge that you can make taxable sales within your state. Your state tax ID also allows you to make non-taxable *purchases*.

Books are generally considered a taxable product. For a publisher, books are usually considered "tangible personal property purchased for resale."

It's important to point out that a taxable sale only occurs *once* when reselling a printed book. The printer does not collect sales tax from you. You're purchasing the books for *resale*, and they're exempt from sales tax to you. This is true even if the printer is in your state.

Some printers require you to send them a seller's permit or some other evidence that you're exempt from paying sales tax. This applies if the printer resides in the same state as you or if the printer has business locations in your state.

In Minnesota, for example, you'd send Form ST3 which is a "Certificate of Exemption." Your state will have its own procedure. A copy of a reseller's permit or a copy of a certificate of exemption gives the printer evidence that the sale was non-taxable. Or, more correctly, it shows that you've assumed responsibility for collecting the sales tax upon resale of the books. Of course, few people purchase 5,000 copies of a single book for personal use, so it could be argued it's rather obvious the purchase was made for resale!

Similarly, if a wholesaler, such as Ingram or Baker & Taylor, or a retailer, such as Borders or Barnes & Noble, purchases a book from you, you do not need to collect sales tax from them. They'll resell the book to the final retail customer and collect sales tax. They'll also remit that sales tax to the proper state. You don't have to take any action. So, if all your sales are made to wholesalers, distributors, retailers, and people who are in the business of reselling your books, you won't need to collect any sales tax yourself.

However, selling books to individual customers is extremely profitable, so you'll probably want to be set up to make individual sales. Remember, the typical discount to bookstores is about 40% and the typical discount to wholesalers and distributors is 55%. When you sell direct to an individual customer, you collect 100% of the retail price of the book, which is much, much better!

At the same time you make a sale to an individual person in your state, you must also collect your state's sales tax. That sales tax *isn't* part of the book's price. It's calculated as some percentage of the book's price, and the collected money is only held by you until it must be remitted to your state. Because you're only collecting this money and holding it for the state, sales tax usually isn't added to a company's revenue. Collected sales tax isn't revenue to your company.

Keep good records of which sales are taxable, so you know how much is owed to your state! If you only make a few taxable sales a year, your state might only require you to file a sales tax return annually. But, what if sales explode?

Occasionally, a publisher is doing very well and making many sales. Because the publisher needs more books to sell, the publisher sometimes has used most of her cash to reprint more books. Then, at the end of the year, the publisher doesn't have the cash on hand to pay the sales tax. That's a very bad situation. Don't let it happen! Keep good records. At a certain level of sales, your state will want you to remit sales tax more often.

Sales tax is one example of a cash outflow that can sneak up on you. You think you're doing well and have enough cash to cover your expenses, but you've failed to account for some expense you've incurred. Sales tax isn't formally an expense. It's something you collect for the state. You're only a pawn in the process! But, you need to write a check to the state or make an electronic deposit and that takes money in your bank, so it affects your cash flow!

Remember: Sales tax isn't included in revenue. It isn't an expense. It's only something you collect and remit to your state according to your state's rules.

Incidentally, we should point out that *you* can also collect certificates of exemption and copies of resale permits from business customers to show that sales made to your business customers are non-taxable.

Suppose you're audited by your state's tax department. If they look at a record of your sales and notice non-taxable sales made in your state, they may want to see resale permits for those customers. Often, the auditor will give you a certain period of time to produce any needed documentation, and you can request the proper reseller documentation needed from larger, established resellers when, and if, you're asked for it.

For example, we all know that big stores, such as Barnes & Noble and Borders, and the bigger distributors, such as Ingram and Baker & Taylor, are reselling books. Your state government should probably accept that those sales are non-taxable! Again, asking your state and collecting the proper documentation are the safest policies.

But, what about other places? How do we know that "Happy Joe's Books" is a bookstore just because he claims to be one? Maybe, Happy Joe's an individual who orders books directly from publishers for his own amusement or to try to get a discount. Or, maybe, Happy

Joe resells books and doesn't bother to collect sales tax. How do we know?

Now, I know what you're thinking. This should be Happy Joe's problem. If Happy Joe says he's exempt, the state government should go after him for not paying sales tax! It seems it shouldn't involve you at this point. Well, if Happy Joe's a bit too happy and spends all his money and goes bankrupt, the state government might just decide to go after someone else in the sale's chain for the owed sales tax. That someone could be you!

Further, what if Happy Joe claims he never resold the books, but was a retail customer? Or, what if he claims it was his understanding that you remitted the sales tax? Then, it might look as if it were *your* responsibility to collect the sales tax! Collecting certificates of exemption or copies of resale permits proves that you were informed the sales were non-taxable. You're not responsible for the sales tax at that point, and the government can't justifiably go after you for it!

The above scenario is very rare, and many publishers don't bother to collect the resale documentation from bookstores and wholesalers in their states. But, I wanted you to know about why such documentation is typically requested by people making non-taxable sales to your company. The key point is that, if a product is taxable, your state wants someone to collect the sales tax for it. Reseller permits prevent everyone from pointing the finger at each other and saying, "I thought he collected it!"

Sales tax is based upon where the purchaser resides, where the seller resides, and where the sale is deemed to have been made. In Minnesota, sales tax is based upon a *taxable sale being made in Minnesota*. A Minnesota company making sales to retail customers in Minnesota must collect sales tax from its customers. Most states are similar. Here 'retail sales' means a sale to a final individual customer who purchases the book for his or her own use. It doesn't require the sale to be made in a retail store!

If an individual customer from your state buys a book, you'll need to collect sales tax for your state at the current sales tax rate. There might also be local sales taxes applied to a sale. For example, in

Minnesota, Saint Paul has a small sales tax for sales made in Saint Paul.

Depending upon your sales volume, you'll file sales tax returns and remit sales tax on a monthly, quarterly, or annual basis.

For Minnesota, if the sale is made to a non-Minnesota resident, you're not required to collect sales tax for an online or direct-mail sale, as long as the product is delivered to an address in another state. This is true in many states. You probably won't have to collect sales tax for retail sales made to customers in other states when the order is shipped to another state.

Because of the Internet's important role in future commerce, the future of sales tax issues related to online sales is subject to change and is in heated debate. Suppose an online store has only one business location in a state that doesn't have sales tax. That company doesn't have to collect state sales tax from any individual purchaser, regardless of the state from which the purchaser orders. If a store with retail locations in all the states makes a sale, that retailer must *always* collect sales tax.

Thus, retailers with locations in all fifty states feel it's unfair to force them to collect sales tax while Internet stores don't have to. The non-taxableness of Internet sales is viewed as an unfair competitive advantage to the online store, because the overall price of the book to the customer is less.

Unless the customer's state is in some sort of weird partnership with your state that says each state will collect sales tax for the other state, when interstate sales are made, and remit it to said state, you don't have to worry about collecting sales tax for sales to customers in other states. To keep you informed of the changing complications, some state departments of revenue have free newsletters that discuss nothing but sales tax. Ask your state about any such sales tax newsletters. They're not the most entertaining newsletters, but they're useful.

The general rule I follow is to ask your state what its rules are and follow them! You must be in compliance with your own state. It will tell you when you must collect sales tax. On my website, I have links to state resources that may help you: http://www.thinkinglike.com/ State-by-State-Business-Resources.html

Always get such information from the horse's mouth—your state. Most states also have booklets that will tell you all you need to know about sales tax in your state.

Some states may actually have passed legislation requiring sellers in all other states to collect sales tax when sales are made for products delivered to that state. This is a good example of a bad law. Even is such a law exists, 99.9999% of the sellers in other states don't know about it, will never know about it, and, even if they knew about it, probably wouldn't care. Compliance with such a law is unreasonably burdensome.

It's important to note when I say "your state," I'm assuming your company is only located in one state. If you have offices in multiple states, you must comply with the sales tax regulations for all of those states.

CCNOW.com & Sales Tax On The Internet

Because processing online credit card orders requires a secure server, an online order form, merchant credit card status, and because many websites don't generate a tremendous number of sales, there are companies which provide credit card processing. Ccnow.com is one such company.

When a company, such as ccnow.com, becomes your reseller, typically, you don't need merchant credit card status. Merchant status costs about $100 a year, and there are other fees. Further, if another company provides this service, you don't need to worry about online security of your orders. With ccnow.com, you simply place some simple html code on your web page, and orders are redirected to ccnow.com's secure server. Ccnow.com's commission is about 9% which seems high, but for many websites with modest levels of orders, it's much more cost effective than acquiring merchant credit card status.

Many publishers argue that you really should get merchant status and accept credit card sales because individual customers expect it.

However, unless you sell books directly during seminars or speeches or receive direct phone orders, you probably can forgo merchant status.

Ccnow.com is in a state that doesn't collect sales tax, so ccnow.com doesn't collect it. Period. They have a rationale for this, and I believe it's on their web site. It goes something like this: They're the sale's source because effectively they're selling the product to the customer and buying it from you. I use ccnow for online orders, and, if an order is delivered to a Minnesota address, I know sales tax hasn't been collected, so I deduct the amount from my sale price and send it to the state. Technically, you're suppose to take the sales tax off the top and not count it in with revenue.

Some publishers disagree with me on this one. They won't remit sales tax for sales made to their state if the order comes from an online reseller located in another state. Why pay money you don't have to? That seems reasonable too! And, it saves a bit of money. But be aware that states want this money for final sales made within your state, and, at some point in the future, might come collecting. If you set up your own online shopping cart, you can calculate sales tax based upon the customer's state.

With states clamoring for what they feel is due them in sales tax, with the floorspace retailers fighting the tax-free nature of Internet sales, and with the growing importance of online sales, we'll see future changes (and, hopefully, simplification!) in how sales tax is dealt with for online sales.

Sales Tax And Book Design Services

Make it a point to check explicitly with your state's department of revenue to see if you're required to pay sales tax (and/or use tax discussed below) on book design services. Many states have publications about how sales tax works for printing and advertising in the state.

Suppose, for example, you pay a cover designer $1,000. Does your state treat the publisher as the end user of that service and demand sales tax? Or, does your state accept that the design is being incorporated into a product for resale and, thus, is sales tax exempt?

The same question should be asked about advertising services: Does your state collect sales tax on advertising services or not? Knowing where your state stands is important because you don't want to be charged extra for sales tax, if it isn't required.

Use Tax

Now, just because no one seems to be required to collect sales tax in many cases doesn't mean that a tax isn't due. In Minnesota, we have the use tax system. This means that, if you order something from another state (you're a buyer now, not a seller) and that state doesn't collect sales tax, you're suppose to collect it yourself and remit it to the State of Minnesota. In other words, you pay your own sales tax if no one else collects it, but it's now called a use tax.

Use tax for businesses is important if you order things from out-of-state. One of the first things a state business tax auditor would look for is what you've listed as expenses and from what states those purchases came. If they came from out-of-state and no use tax has been paid, you're in trouble. You obviously haven't been paying your use tax! (Recently, a big-wig CEO avoided paying millions of dollars in sales/use tax for fine art he purchased. He's being sent to prison.)

I hope this helps. In short, ask your state! Follow what your state says. Don't worry about what's happening in other states, unless you have some indication the law's changed. Don't forget to pay your business use tax, if required by your state. Again, I want to emphasize that this is only my personal understanding of sales tax issues. Check with your state!

Deductible Costs In Publishing. Inventory Accounting.

Many self-publishers are writers and creative individuals who aren't familiar with business. Hence, some of the most common questions new self-publishers ask focus upon the small business aspects of self-publishing. This chapter will teach you a bit about accounting and deductible costs in publishing.

Cash Basis Accounting vs. Accrual Basis Accounting

Most people are familiar with cash basis accounting, because that's the way most people manage their personal finances.

Typically, a person has a checkbook and receives a paycheck every other week. When the person receives his paycheck, he makes an addition to the money in the checkbook. Then, he goes shopping, writes checks, and subtracts the amount of money for each check as it's written. The checkbook serves as a proxy for the person's income and expenses.

Notice that income and expenses are tied directly to the availability of cash in the checkbook. Cash is received when income is reported—a deposit is made. Cash is subtracted when expenses are paid—a check is written. This is a case of cash flow coinciding with income and expenses.

However, suppose the person uses a charge card to purchase a $200 sweater. Most people don't keep a record of outgoing personal expenses that will be paid in the future. They might 'remember' that they charged $200 and 'know' that they need to keep $200 available from their next paycheck to pay for the sweater. But, by and large, no personal record is made of the money owed. People let the charge card companies do that. Similarly, no record is made of money that will be received until the money is received.

Cash-basis accounting reports income when cash is received and reports expenses when cash is paid—just as your personal checkbook accounts for expenses and income.

For many small businesses, cash-basis accounting is adequate and allowed. But, for most businesses, cash-basis accounting isn't the best way to track income and expenses. Also, many businesses are required to keep their accounting books on an accrual basis or a hybrid basis, which is part accrual and part cash. *Businesses that have inventory are required to use accrual accounting for at least the inventory from a tax standpoint.*

Consider a publisher who writes a check and purchases a laser printer for $800 to help him proof his book's layout. The publisher writes another check for $3—$1 for ten pens used in editing and $2 for 500 sheets of paper for the laser printer. Then, the publisher prints 3,000 books for $6,000 and writes a check for the books to the book printer. Then, 1,000 books are sold in the first month for a total of $15,000. But, this money isn't received until 90 days later.

What does pure cash-basis accounting tell us? Well, we have an expense of $800, an expense of $3, and it looks like an 'expense' of $6,000. But, no income is received, so that it looks as if we have no income. We might think we have a total expense of $6,803 and a total income of zero. It looks like the publisher is doing quite poorly if everything were evaluated on a purely cash basis. This is wrong.

In actuality, we own a printer and 2,000 books and we are owed money. Those items are assets to our business. They have value to us. *Items purchased for resale, such as inventory, are carried as assets and can only be expensed when the assets are sold.*

Some assets which have a lifetime of over one year are also carried as assets and 'expensed' or 'depreciated' over a number of years. This means that a certain portion of the long-term asset's value is deducted each year as an expense until the total value of the deductions equals the total purchase value of the asset.

The IRS does allow a business to deduct a certain level of *long-term assets* in a given year (IRS Section 179 Deduction. This does not apply to inventory!), so we'll assume that we will deduct the full cost of the printer ($800) as an expense in the current period.

We also have sales of $15,000 even though we haven't been paid for the sales yet. So, our proper expenses are $800 for the printer, $3 for office supplies, and $2,000 in cost-of-goods-sold expenses. Cost-of-goods-sold (cogs) is the purchase value of the inventory we've sold during the period. Our books have a per-unit cost of $2, and we've sold 1,000 of them. So, the cost of our goods sold is $2,000.

Thus, our income/expense results are more adequately described as:

$15,000 Sales
-    2,000 Cogs Expense
_____

$13,000 Gross Profit
-        803 Expenses Not Accounted For In Cogs.
_____

  $12,197

Thus, we've done quite well and earned $12,197 over the period. A pure cash-basis accounting (which would not be allowed by the IRS!) seems to show a loss of $6,803. Because we will likely owe taxes on the profit and because the IRS expects us to make estimated tax payments on our profits, it's crucial to know how well our business is doing on an accrual basis. There's a world of difference between thinking we've lost $6,803 and will be able to deduct $6,803 from our taxes and owing taxes on profits of $12,197! We don't want to wind up owing money we don't have at the end of the year to the IRS!

The above is actually an example of an *income statement*, sometimes also known as an income-expense statement or a profit-loss statement. We can also track when money leaves our company (cash outflow) and when money enters our company (cash inflow), and that's called a *cash flow statement*. Our cash flow statement shows we have a *negative* cash flow during the period of $6,803.

Let's assume the time frame in question is one quarter—three months. We have created an income statement and a cash flow statement for our first quarter. We can also create a balance sheet, which is a statement of our assets and liabilities. Suppose we have $100 in our checkbook. We also have 2,000 books worth $4,000. We are owed $15,000. So, we have an accounts receivable asset of $15,000. We don't owe any money to anyone, i.e., our liabilities are zero. Thus, our total assets are valued at $19,100.

Notice that the printer and the office supplies, which were already expensed, have no asset value. While the IRS requires businesses with inventory to use accrual basis accounting for inventory, smaller expenses are usually treated on a cash basis. And, items purchased and expensed immediately have no stated asset value.

For example, suppose we've used only one of the ten pens purchased and 250 sheets of the laser paper. Each pen has a value of $0.10, so we still have 'pen' assets of $0.90. Half the value of the paper remains and that's worth $1. So, if everything is carried on pure accrual, we have office assets of $1.90. We could be even more extreme and look at the ink in the pen we've been using and notice that half of it remains. Thus, we haven't even used one pen, but only half a pen. So, office assets are truly $1.95.

That level of accrual detail is obviously not worth doing and even the IRS won't force us to carry everything down to the pages of office paper and ink in our pens on an accrual basis! Small expenses should be written off immediately!

The basic logic behind reporting income and expenses on an accrual basis is that income should not be reported when it's received, but rather it should be recorded when it's *earned*. Expenses should not be recorded when they are paid. Rather, they should be recorded when they are *incurred*.

It should be clear why the IRS requires accrual accounting for inventory. If we could deduct the value of inventory immediately when it's purchased, we'd have a way to avoid paying taxes on much of our profits or we would at least be able to defer that tax into the future.

Having inventory, your business will be on an accrual basis or a hybrid method where inventory is accounted for on an accrual basis and most other things are accounted for on a cash basis. For your inventory, use accrual.

To help you understand small business accounting issues, I highly recommend *Small Time Operator: How To Start Your Own Small Business, Keep Your Books, Pay Your Taxes, And Stay Out Of Trouble!* by Bernard Kamoroff and *Keeping The Books: Basic Record-Keeping and Accounting For The Small Business, Plus Up-to-Date Tax Information* by Linda Pinson and Jerry Jinnett.

A great deal about basic taxation and accounting can be learned from free IRS booklets available either on paper or in Adobe Acrobat reader (PDF) format, which can be downloaded from the IRS website (Forms and Publications Section of irs.gov). Some of the more useful IRS booklets are: Publication 334, *Tax Guide for Small Business*; Publication 535, *Business Expenses*; Publication 538, *Accounting Periods and Methods*.

Also, our small business website, thinkinglike.com, has links to tax and accounting information. Finally, you'll notice a state-by-state section of links to state government resources about starting a business on thinkinglike.com. Many state revenue departments in association with the IRS hold free classes to teach the basics of business taxation. Consult your local Department of Revenue for information about enrolling in one of these classes. The classes dealing with employment taxes are especially useful if you hire employees.

More About COGS And Inventory Valuation

Cost of goods sold and inventory valuation are sufficiently important that they deserve their own discussion. *You must know your per-unit book cost to price your book effectively.*

In addition to the cost of printing your book, other costs can also be added into the value of inventory (capitalized). The IRS does allow some flexibility as to what must be capitalized and what can be expensed immediately. But, you can only choose one option—either the expense is deducted immediately, or it's added to inventory and deducted as the units sell, never both! When in doubt, the path least likely to get you into trouble with the IRS is capitalizing the expense into inventory and, then, deducting it with cogs as the units sell. That option often doesn't maximize your tax benefit, however. In addition, capitalizing certain costs into inventory gives you the best measure of your true per-unit book costs.

Suppose you print 3,000 books for $6,000. The books are shipped to you from the printer. You pay $300 in shipping charges. You have a cover designed for your book. Your cover designer charges you $1,000. You purchase a barcode for the book for $12, and you purchase a special font for your book cover for $30. You also purchase a book of ten ISBN numbers for $200. You have a photograph scanned and touched up for the cover. The cost is $50.

Let's lump all one-time costs together and look at them. The cover design, the bar code, the photograph work, and the font are clearly one-time expenses associated with this specific book. The ISBN is a bit tricky because you have ten ISBN numbers which are good for ten books.

There is considerable debate among small publishers as to whether book design costs should be immediately deducted when they're incurred or whether they should be capitalized into the cost of your first press run. I tend to favor conservatism. I capitalize these costs into the cost of the first press run.

Other publishers do deduct them immediately. That tends to maximize the tax benefit. So, you might want to check with your accountant and follow his or her advice about which costs to capitalize and which to deduct immediately. You're less likely to get into trouble with the IRS if you follow an accountant's advice. Unfortunately, some accountants don't seem to understand business accounting for small publishers.

For the ISBN's, let's assume you decide to carry nine of the numbers as an asset. You record an asset of $180 for the nine, *unused* ISBN numbers. As each number is used, you'll transfer that asset value to the cost associated with the design of the book. Because you're printing one book now, one ISBN number is being used, and it has a value of $20. That $20 will be included with the one-time design costs of your book.

The total one-time design costs of the book are $1,112. This is the amount that some publishers will expense immediately. But, we will add it to the value of inventory. The shipping charges should also be added to inventory. Thus, the total value of inventory is $1,112 + $6,000 + $300 = $7,412. Thus, the first press run has a per-unit cost of $7,412/3,000 = $2.47.

Other publishers argue that shipping costs should be expensed immediately and not capitalized into the inventory. Again, expensing shipping charges immediately leads to the largest immediate tax deduction. Even though shipping charges do not seem to be an "asset" in the same sense that your books are an asset, shipping charges effectively increase the per unit cost of your books. This is effectively no different than paying a slightly higher per unit printing cost for the books. Check with your accountant to determine if you must capitalize shipping charges or if it's better to expense them immediately.

We assume that you receive all 3,000 books. It's always important to count cartons and be sure the total agrees with the number the printer says were shipped. Sometimes a carton will be "missing." You want to be sure to let your printer know and make a note of that when you sign for the books. If you only receive 2,990 books, your per unit cost is slightly higher—$2.48.

Incidentally, if you have a good printer and if you have any trouble with the shipper, your printer will be able to help you immensely. Printers, typically, get quotes from several carriers and choose the least expensive one. Often, however, you pay this cost directly to the shipper.

Always be sure to ask for an estimate from the printer of the shipping costs to get the books from the printer to your company. That not only affects your per unit costs—printers closer to your company will be slightly less expensive when freight is considered—but also, sometimes, shippers will try to overbill you.

If the shipper quotes $500 and that's the value the printer returns to you, but, then, the shipper tries to bill you $700, don't take it sitting down! Tell the shipper you were quoted $500. If the shipper gives you any fuss about that then call your representative at the printer and tell him or her. Often, your printer's representative will call the shipper, and you'll pay the lower rate.

Some shippers will try to bid low to get the business, but then try to up the price to the publisher. Remember, most publishers don't use shippers nearly as often as printers do, and they often don't choose the shipper. So, some shippers don't care about a small publisher as a customer. It's a different story with printers who represent *big business* to the shipper. If the shipper is playing games, the printer needs to know! The shipper is counting upon a lack of communication between the printer and the publisher to add to their profits and to charge much more than they quoted the printer.

Often, if you try to point out the difference between the quoted shipping price and the cost the shipper is trying to bill you to the shipper, you'll just get the run around: "Oh, no. That charge applies to you, and we can't get rid of it. No way. No how. Never. Sorry. Can't do it. Sorry. Pay the full bill!"

But, a call to the printer's representative will usually result in: "I'm sorry. You're right. The cost is only $500."

If the carton count doesn't agree with the printer's outgoing count, that's something you also want to be sure the printer knows. If books are missing, it's almost always due to a five-finger discount somewhere along the shipping line. It's very seldom due to a miscount at the printer.

Pornography books, so I'm told, are especially susceptible to being "lost" in transit. Most printers slap labels on every box naming the title inside. So, if you've got a title such as *Erotic Women Of The East*, you might want to tell your printer to use some other label on the cartons, such as EWOE or *An Introduction To Algebra*.

Getting back to our scenario, we've calculated the per-unit cost of each book at $2.47. For each copy you sell, that's the cogs *per unit*. That's the number to use from a tax standpoint. However, you should also calculate the cost per unit for each copy *excluding* the one-time design costs and also allowing for any one-time printer set-up fees.

One-time printer set-up fees, making the plate, for example, might be $700. Thus, upon reprint, your cost might be ($6,000 - $700 + $300)/3,000 = $1.87. Notice, you *always* add the inbound shipping charges into the per unit cost, because you'll pay shipping each time you have books sent to you. This number gives you a measure of your per-unit cost upon a *reprint*. It's nice to know you'll earn more money per unit if your book is reprinted!

Many times, it's easiest to just figure your total cogs for a period as:

(Per-Unit Cost)(Number of Copies Sold During The Period)

For example, if you sell 1,000 books, your total cogs is (1,000)($2.47) = $2,470. Be careful to pay attention to any *round off error*. Maybe, your actual per unit cost is $2.4729. When worked out that represents a difference of $2.90 for 1,000 books. So, carry the extra decimal places.

The other way that cost-of-goods-sold is calculated is *without regard to per-unit cost*. When you figure cost-of-goods-sold for tax purposes, it usually works something like this:

Starting Inventory
+ Purchases In Year
  +/- Adjustments
- Ending Inventory
_____

cogs

We could add inbound shipping charges to either the "Purchases" or else to the "Adjustments." In our above example:

Starting Inventory = $0
Purchases = $6,000 + $300
Adjustments = $1,112 (book design costs capitalized into inventory)

Ending Inventory is calculated as the value of the inventory at the end of the period. Here, we have 2,000 copies remaining. The original per unit cost is $2.4706. So, the value of ending inventory is $4,941.20. Hence, the cogs for the period is $2,470.80

LIFO vs. FIFO

There are two standard ways of accounting for book inventory. "Lower of cost or market" isn't typically used in publishing. Inventory is almost always valued at cost. The two accounting conventions used are LIFO and FIFO. LIFO is most common. LIFO is Last-In-First-Out. FIFO is First-In-First-Out.

Suppose you have a press run of 1,000 books, and the cost is $2,000. Then, you have another press run of 1,000 books and the cost is $3,000. If you sell all 2,000 books, the total cost-of-goods-sold is clearly $5,000 for that title.

But, what if you only sell 1,500 books? Which per-unit book cost should be used? Here's where LIFO and FIFO are used.

On a LIFO basis, the inventory last in is considered first out. The books last in have a per-unit cost of $3.00, and we've consumed all of them. The next 500 books come from previous inventory and have a cost of $1,000. Thus, our cogs is $4,000 on LIFO. And, the 500 books remaining in inventory have a value of $1,000.

With FIFO: The books in first are assumed sold first. So, the first 1,000 books sold are the $2.00 per unit books for a cogs of $2,000. The next 500 books come from the 'newest' books on hand and have a cogs of $1,500. So, the total cogs is $3,500. The total value of inventory is $1,500.

LIFO and FIFO are only accounting conventions. The books from the different press runs might be fully indistinguishable, so LIFO doesn't mean you must sell physically older inventory. You could be shipping the newer books and be on LIFO accounting.

Because printing costs tend to rise and because we probably want the highest cogs to get the greatest immediate tax benefit, many publishers prefer LIFO.

Some new publishers wonder why they shouldn't just average the value of the inventory rather than use LIFO ($5,000 divided by 2,000 books for an average per unit cost of $2.50). This actually *complicates* things, because we don't want to re-average our existing inventory each time we have a new press run.

Deductible Books

In the publishing industry, it's common to send out complimentary copies to syndicated columnists and newspaper book reviewers. Those copies are *tax deductible* because they are a legitimate marketing expense. The purpose in giving these copies away is to try to generate more sales.

There is much debate in the small press community about whether or not individual copies of books given away to friends and family are a justifiable tax-deductible expense. I tend to believe that they aren't. Some publishers argue that any word-of-mouth is good for a book and copies given away help to generate publicity and word-of-mouth, no matter to whom they're given. Hence, they argue they're deductible.

Books given to your authors as complimentary copies are a deductible expense to the publishing company. If you're both author and publisher, and you (as publisher) give yourself (as author) free books, it's a bit tricky. Clearly, the IRS doesn't want you to give yourself 1,000 books and deduct them immediately! So, keep any number of complimentary author copies reasonably small. Ask your personal tax accountant if you must report the small number of books you give yourself as taxable income. You might just want to allow yourself, as a self-published author, to buy books at cost from your publishing company, if you wish to give them away to friends and family.

Deduct The Cost And Nothing But The Cost!

Every year or so, on the Publish-L discussion list, a question appears which goes something like this: "Can I deduct the full retail price of the books given away as complimentary copies or can I only deduct the actual cost?"

Only deduct the *actual cost*. Nothing more. Don't add the value of your time or anything else to the deductible cost, unless you're also reporting that value of time as income!

You can write off the cost of review copies because they are a legitimate promotional expense. You can write off only the actual cost to acquire and send the copies, i.e., printing costs plus amortized shipping from the printer, plus whatever postage you spent to send out the review copy, etc. Those are your legitimate expenses.

If you think about it, if the IRS would allow a deduction for the full retail price, you could print only 100 copies, price them at a million dollars a copy, send out a review copy or two a year, and never pay taxes again! The IRS doesn't allow this "review copy tax dodge."

So, if your retail price is $16.95 per unit, but your actual per unit cost is $4.00, your tax deduction is only $4 for each copy given away in promotion.

Another question many new publishers have is where to report the deductible copies given away in promotion on their tax forms. Publishers have different opinions here. Some argue it should be reported on the "marketing expense" line, which is logical. But, I've never liked that because it requires that you also adjust inventory levels to explain the decrease in inventory. Why not just let the deductible complimentary copies flow through cost-of-goods-sold? That's easiest. Either way, the overall deduction is the same.

Whichever way you do it, don't let the deductible complimentary copies flow through cogs and then *also* report them as "marketing expense" on another line of your tax return. If you do this, you'd be deducting them *twice*. You may *not* deduct the value of your complimentary copies given away *twice*!

In addition to complimentary copies given away, missing books will add to your cogs which is an expense. Books lost in outbound shipping or stolen from your warehouse are tax deductible as ordinary business expenses.

If you desire, you can always include a note on your tax return that explains that cogs includes xxx books damaged or missing, xxx books sent as complimentary copies that were marketing expense, etc.

With a missing shipment, no sale is made because the goods aren't delivered. So, you can record the sale with the second shipment if the books are resent. There are other ways to account for this, but, ultimately, lost books are deductible as a justifiable business expense.

If you measure cogs as:

Starting Inventory
+ Purchases In Year
  +/- Adjustments
- Ending Inventory

---

cogs

you'll see that complimentary copies and missing books add naturally to your cogs expense. Suppose, rather than an Ending Inventory of 2,000 copies, you count your inventory and only have 1,900 copies. Then, your cogs is higher by the extra 100 missing copies.

Using your original per-unit cost of $2.4706, we see the ending inventory has a value of $4,694.14. As before, the value of Starting Inventory + Purchases In Year +/- Adjustments is $7,412.00. Thus, your cogs for the period is $2,717.86.

If you compare this cogs to the value previously calculated, you see the difference is $2,717.86 - $2,470.80 = $247.06 which represents the value of 100 copies lost or given away. Those copies weren't actually "sold" even though they flow through cogs. Part is marketing expense and part is missing or damaged copy expense. But, it's common to allow damaged inventory to flow through cost-of-goods-sold, so I don't see why complimentary copies can't do likewise.

Suppose you examine your list of complimentary copies sent out and see that you only sent out 40 copies. What happened to the other 60 copies? Assume you don't have any damaged copies that can't be sold to explain the difference. That's a serious problem. This is the reason why actual inventory counts at regular intervals should be made. At the very least, an annual inventory count should be made.

You want to know if books are disappearing from your warehouse. Theft is a serious small business problem. Thieves don't just steal your profits, they steal the value of your inventory. With typical net profit margins of only 10% in many industries and gross profit margins of 30%, this means that to make up for the value of one lost or stolen product, you need to sell about *seven* additional products. Safeguard your inventory! Fortunately, with books, the situation isn't quite as bad as that because books are often marked up by factors of five to ten.

If you ship your books USPS (United States Post Office) media mail rate, you should place little stickers that say "Media Mail, Return Service Requested" on your packages. Many people don't know this, but without such a sticker, undeliverable media mail isn't returned to the sender. For books that have production costs comparable to postage, the savings aren't significant in having the books returned to you. But, you need to know if books are undeliverable. For full case shipments of books, if you use USPS media mail, be sure to spend a little extra money and get a delivery confirmation.

Other Deductible Costs In Publishing

Many other costs are tax deductible in publishing. As a rule, any expense that is 'ordinary' and 'necessary' in the course of running your business is tax deductible. If the cost is incurred by your business as the result of trying to do business, it's probably deductible. I refer you to *Small Time Operator: How To Start Your Own Small Business, Keep Your Books, Pay Your Taxes, And Stay Out Of Trouble!* by Bernard Kamoroff for a more detailed discussion.

Some people try to claim personal expenses as deductible business expenses, and some pretty off-the-wall expenses find their way into tax returns. My favorite comes from the Dilbert award which went to the CEO who tried to deduct the cost of voodoo dolls so that he could hex his competition. Don't try to cheat Uncle Sam on taxes by trying to deduct personal, non-business expenses. If you're caught, you'll not only pay back taxes, but fines and penalties.

Travel And Entertainment

Travel and entertainment expenses are two categories that tend to draw IRS audits, even if you aren't abusing the expenses. This is because these categories are so often abused in many other industries.

Yet, travel to promote books and some entertainment, such as buying a reporter lunch, are fully deductible business expenses, and you have every right to deduct them. Just be sure to keep your receipts and make a note as to why the expense is deductible so you don't forget.

For example, if you fly to Hawaii, it might appear you're on vacation. But, if you're there for a speaking engagement and have scheduled book signings, part, if not all, of that trip is deductible. See IRS Publication 463, which discusses travel and entertainment expenses.

Book Production

Cover Design, Book Layout—Costs, Options & Do-It-Yourself

Once your book is written and edited, it must be converted into a format that can be printed and bound by your book printer. While you could use Microsoft Word or another word processor to create a printable book, the results will be better if you use a full page layout program or hire a talented freelancer to do your book's layout.

For example, if you examine documents with justified text created in a real page layout program, you'll notice that the justification is expertly handled. Justified text created by a word processor usually looks poor, because letter spacing isn't adjustable and the text flow isn't as controlled. You don't want factors like that creeping into your book.

Doing the interior book design and layout is very easy, so you might want to do that yourself. But, of course, you could also outsource interior book design.

Most experienced small publishers believe cover design should be outsourced to experienced freelancers. A great cover is important for book marketing. If you hope to get your books into bookstores, you'll *need* a great cover.

Experienced cover designers typically charge $1,000 to about $1,500 for a cover design. It's always a good idea to get feedback from other publishers about any freelancer. Is the person easy and enjoyable to work with? How well did their cover turn out? Did the cover designer offer you multiple options and was he/she willing to incorporate your ideas? Does the cover designer have experience?

Examine some samples of the designer's work. I'm always skeptical of cover designers who don't have websites showing many examples of their work. Examples that correspond to published books are best. That way you can contact the publishers and ask about their experience with the cover designer.

Award-winning cover designer and owner of TLC Graphics, Tamara Dever offers this advice when working with a professional cover designer:

> Expect to sign a written contract with the designer. Be wary of working with a designer who doesn't use a contract. The contract should cover exactly what will be produced for you, the timeline for production, and the agreed-upon cost, often a flat fee of roughly $700 to $1,500 and more. A big issue that should be spelled out in the contract is who will own the final artwork. Unless the contract specifically states that ownership is being transferred *(and this is rare)*, the designer will automatically own the cover design he or she creates.

While the designer typically retains ownership of the cover design, the publisher usually has the right to use the cover forever. Dever also suggests giving your cover designer at least three full months to develop your cover. For more information about hiring and working with a cover designer, see Dever's article, *Good Covers Sell Books* at www.TLCgraphics.com.

Incidentally, some new authors and publishers who are also artists turn to cover design as a service they offer other publishers. This is a way for them to supplement their income, and many freelancers make a great living just designing book covers.

With a bit of experience, I feel a *very basic cover* can be designed relatively quickly. Most publishers disagree with me on this point, but I tend to recommend trying to design your own cover, even if you choose not to use it! If nothing else, you'll learn a lot about book design, and you'll start to pay attention to design and production issues you probably neglected before.

On the other hand, the cost of the cover design isn't that much when you consider that it's a one-time expense. Once you have a great cover, it can serve for decades and last through tens of thousands or even hundreds of thousands of book sales.

Book covers appear deceptively simple to design. This is because good design shouldn't call attention to itself. It just makes you want to buy the book!

Don't be misled by what seems a high price for a cover design. At a cost of $1,200, a cover design might seem expensive. But, if you're making a profit of $4 per book, that represents only 300 book sales. And, a great cover will help sell far more copies than that! A great cover might be the difference between a bestseller that earns you hundreds of thousands of dollars and a book that you remainder for $1 a copy. *In this way, a professional cover design is a great investment, because it will help generate more book sales.*

In conclusion, if you want to get your books into bookstores, if you're aiming to have a bestseller, and if you have a relatively large target market, hire a professional cover designer. If you're producing a book with a very limited niche market, you might want to consider doing-it-yourself. If you publish other authors, you must always assure the cover is of the highest quality.

Of Text And Type And Postscript

You should write your book with a standard word processor, such as Word. The spell checking features and editing features of Word, Wordperfect, and other word processors are usually far superior to the text editing capability of page layout programs. But, do the final book layout in a layout program.

Incidentally, many people use the fonts Times or Times New Roman 12-point type as their default type for their word processor. Both are highly readable. If you plan to use Times for the body text in your book, you should set the default font to Times in your word processor.

Times is usually a standard postscript font (postscript is discussed later). It comes free with most layout software and postscript laser printers. You'll have to pay extra to use Times New Roman! When you place your word processor text into page layout software, you don't want non-postscript fonts to be imported.

If you find that you need a postscript version of a font, you can buy one online from Adobe.com. Postscript fonts cost about $30 from Adobe. Adobe has thousands upon thousands of type faces.

While I recommend new publishers stick to postscript fonts commonly available from adobe.com to minimize the likelihood of errors, some fonts are custom designed for companies. Some artists (see chank.com, for example) earn money designing new fonts. Font design is yet another way artists have found to earn extra money.

Typically, one page of 8-1/2 by 11 text in Times 12-point flows into one and a half pages of Times 12-point, when laid out in a 6 by 9 book (6x9). So, if you're trying to write a 200-page book, 6x9, and you plan to use Times 12-point as the body text, then, dividing 200 by 1.5, we see you need to write about 133 pages on your word processor. If you've already written 200 pages on your word processor, a 6x9 book will be about 300 pages.

If you decide you want a slightly smaller type and decide to change the type to Times 11-point, your book will shrink by about 20%. These conversion values are sometimes useful in estimating how long a book will be, based upon the length of a word processor document.

Adobe Pagemaker 7.0 (or, the latest version) is probably the best choice for page layout for publishers who wants to do it themselves. Quark Express is another option, but that program is a bit pricier and, I'm told, has a higher learning curve. Many community colleges have reasonably-priced classes teaching Pagemaker and Quark. You might want to enroll in one of these courses if you plan to do page layout yourself.

Your book printer should be able to give you detailed information about setting up your files so that they are compatible with the printer's imagesetter. Be sure to get instructions from your printer *before* you begin laying out your book to prevent needing to redo things.

Suppose you lay out a chapter of your book and find the original 'document setup' options are incorrect, or you wish to change them. While you can trivially go to 'document setup' and change the options to make them agree with your wishes, this can cause difficulties, because the text might flow differently under different options. And, you might not notice the problems until your printer tells you about them. As a general rule, the earlier you catch problems, the less costly and time-consuming they are to fix. Get your file setup right from the start!

You should create a template document and work from that to eliminate any inconsistency. Each time you open a template, it will create a new file into which you can place text and graphics. Before creating your files, you'll usually need to install the appropriate print driver that matches your book printer's imagesetter. For example, you can install a print driver for the Linotronic 530, a common imagesetter even though you don't have your computer hooked up to a Linotronic 530. Set it up so that it prints to a file. Then, when you create digital files for the book printer, go to "File..Print...Write Postscript to File." Be sure you examine all options and verify that they're set as your book printer has instructed.

Many printers will test your files for free. You should take advantage of that to assure your files work. Also, examine your printer's website for more information. Thomson-Shore is particularly easy to work with for new publishers.

Postscript, The Language Of Printers

When we send files to a book printer, the printer usually has an imagesetter that uses the postscript language, which is a language for talking with laser printers and imagesetters. We typically send the book printer postscript files that can be interpreted by the printer's imagesetter. These files typically have a .ps extension. Once a postscript file is created, you can double click it, and if you have Adobe Acrobat Distiller installed (comes free with Pagemaker), it will open and convert the postscript files (.ps) into pdf. Those pdf files are readable by Adobe Acrobat Reader.

Many book printers can image pdf files with little problem. Pdf files are more robust. You can almost think of them as little snapshots of your book's pages. You don't need to be concerned about having non-postscript fonts, for example, if you're supplying pdf files to your book printer. So, pdf appears to be the file format of the future when sending files to printers.

Buy A Postscript Laser Printer For Testing Your Files

Book printers are moving toward working with pdf files directly. Many cheaper laser printers don't support the postscript language. And, many printers that support postscript install drivers for "enhanced" capability which can handle almost anything. Often a postscript driver won't be installed automatically (for most people that's good. If all you want to do is print on your laser printer, use the enhanced drivers, and you can print anything, *including fonts for which you don't have postscript versions*).

But, if you want to check the quality of your pages and be sure they'll image properly, you cannot rely upon the enhanced print drivers to tell you if your files will work in the book printer's imagesetter properly (the "enhanced" drivers will print almost anything). *If you plan to supply postscript files to the book printer, you want to test your files on your PC printer using only postscript drivers, because that's the only capability the book printer's imagesetter will have.*

Your book printer will furnish guidelines about creating postscript or pdf for them. Be sure you set the options as the book printer tells you for printing to file and for distilling.

You don't need a printer (let alone a postscript one) to create pdf files and postscript files. Usually, when creating pdf or postscript, you will go to the "Print" option, but, then, you'll send output not to a printer, but to a file, i.e., you can have the proper driver installed even if you don't have the hardware to use it. Having a printer that handles postscript is necessary to fully test the files and be sure that they will image correctly on a postscript imagesetter. The book printer will usually want you to include a laser proof that exactly matches your digital files. That way they can check pages from their imagesetter against a hard copy they know to be good.

If you are using Pagemaker, I think the safest way to test your files is to print them using the postscript driver directly to your PC printer. Then, create your postscript (.ps). Finally, even if you're sending .ps files, double click on the .ps files, converting them into pdf files, and take one last look at them.

Sweet Sixteen

The magic number of pages in publishing is *sixteen*. Most book printers print large sheets of paper on both sides that are then folded back and forth akin to an Origami bird. Then, those bundles of pages are cut to create a final *group* of pages. Some POD printers only work four pages at a time, but most offset printers use sixteen-page signatures. "Signatures" refer to a group of pages that resulted from folding and cutting one large, printed sheet.

Often, a sixteen-page signature can be cut in half to create an eight-page signature. Ask your book printer how many pages are in their signatures. Your final book should be a multiple of the page number given by the printer, be it four, eight, or sixteen. This is why there are many 240-page books, for example. That represents 15 full sixteen-page signatures. 256 pages represent 16 full sixteen-page signatures.

While cutting a sixteen-page signature to make an eight-page signature isn't usually a problem, it does represent another *step* in the process that can be expected to add to the book's cost. And, extra steps increase the chances of something going wrong.

You would never print a 241-page book. That would require fifteen full signatures and one silly page. That one page would be a problem. You would either edit the book to 240 pages or else add material and bring it to 248 pages. You can always leave a page or two blank at the end of the book. I am personally fond of uncut signatures. I like multiples of sixteen.

Choose Your Cover

The two most common types of books are paperback and hardcover. Paperbacks are sometimes called "perfect" binding. Typically, to produce a paperback, one of the last steps is to cut off a tiny bit from the pages facing the spine. The spine is the back part of the book that holds the pages together. The spine is what you see when you look at a book sitting on a bookshelf.

After cutting the pages, so that each individual page is free, the pages are glued together and to the cover to produce the softcover book.

If you pick up a piece of paper and fold it over several times, you'll notice the folded part near the "spine" bulges out. Some pages of the folded group are farther toward the back of the "spine" while inner pages are pushed away from the "spine." The final cutting to free the pages assures that all pages will be the same distance from the spine and will hold together nicely when glued.

For hardcovers, cutting a bit off the pages facing the spine isn't necessary. In fact, it's not good. If you examine the binding of a quality hardcover, you'll see the actual signatures coming together at the spine. Leaving the signatures together strengthens the book. The Cadillac of all books is the smythe sewn hardcover. That means that the individual signatures are sewn together.

When I produced *Thinking Like An Entrepreneur*, I wanted the highest quality book, so I chose smythe sewn hardcover. Expect to pay, maybe, $2 more per book for hardcover.

The glued hardcover has always seemed a bit silly to me. If you want to produce a high-quality hardcover, *sew* the pages together, so they'll really hold up under intensive use! Librarians love smythe sewn books. Don't just glue a hardcover! Some publishers claim modern glues make smythe sewing unnecessary. I disagree. If you want to make the book less expensively, go to paperback.

Spine Bulk

Spine bulk measures the thickness of the spine of your book, which is also the thickness of the book measured anywhere else.

When you set up your cover for design, you'll want to know the spine bulk, which essentially means knowing the thickness of the paper you're using and the number of pages. Plus, you need to know if you want a hardcover or a softcover.

Many printers have online calculators or free programs you can download to calculate spine bulk. For example, if you go to Thomson-Shore's website, you'll see a free, downloadable program called "Spine Bulk" for calculating spine bulk. That program is nice because it also prints out cover diagrams which show you how to set up your cover in a page-layout program, such as Pagemaker or Quark. I suggest you download that program and print out some diagrams to see how book covers are laid out as one big monolithic page. Ingram's POD Lighting also has cover templates and an online spine bulk calculator.

For softcovers, calculating the thickness of your book is easy. First, decide what kind of paper you'll be using. White paper is less expensive than natural-colored paper. For softcovers, I think white paper also looks better. But, for hardcovers, natural-colored paper has a richer look.

Name That Paper!

As you get more experienced as a publisher, you'll be able to pick up a book at random and guess the paper used. Is that paperback 60# Thor White, or is it 60# Joy White? Is this hardcover done in 60# Glatfelter Offset or 60# Supple Opaque? Or might it be 55# Glatfelter Offset?

Notice I said you'd be able to guess. That's not the same as guessing correctly. When you request a quote from a printer, ask for a paper and cover sampler. The printer will send you the papers it commonly uses, so you'll have an idea of how Thor White differs from Joy White, etc.

Often, the pages they send you are 8-1/2 by 11. When the book is printed in a smaller size, for example, 5 by 8, the pages are smaller and will appear stiffer and of higher quality to many who judge a page by its size. Larger sheets always seem flimsier!

Associated with each paper is a bulk, measured in Pages Per Inch (PPI). PPI measures exactly what you'd think it would. It's the number of pages that add up to one inch in thickness. So, for 60# Thor White, with 440 PPI, 440 pages have a thickness of one inch. 220 pages have a thickness of 1/2 inch. For a paper with 360 PPI, 360 pages of paper have a thickness of one inch. And, so on. A single sheet of paper consists of two pages, front and back, or even and odd page numbers.

To determine the thickness of your book, divide the PPI of the paper into the number of pages to get the book's thickness in inches. For example, if we have a high-bulk paper of 360 PPI and our book is 128 pages in length, the spine bulk of the book is 0.356 inches. If our paper is 440 PPI, the spine bulk of the book is 0.291 inches. If the book is 160 pages and our paper has 360 PPI, its thickness is 0.444 inches.

It's important to know the PPI of the paper you're using to design the spine thickness of the book correctly. Fortunately, several PPI values are quite common, so if you need to switch book printers and have designed your book cover at 440 PPI, that printer probably has a quality paper at 440 PPI.

For softcovers, that's about it. The book's cover isn't that thick. Ask your printer how much you should add to the spine, if anything. But for hardcovers, you must also allow for the thickness of the hardcover when you design the dust jacket.

Of Dust Jackets And Dust

I don't know why the paper wraparound covers to hardcover books are called 'dust jackets.' They certainly don't protect the book from dust! If you produce a hardcover, you want a dust jacket, because they're expected by readers and allow flashier cover designs.

Many publishers suggest printing extra copies of your book covers, either softcovers or hardcover jackets, for use in book promotion. You can include the cover of the book with press kits and in other publicity materials. Plus, for hardcovers, if you accidentally rip a dust jacket and have a supply of extra jackets, you can just add a new jacket to the book and it will be as good as new. Be sure to tell the printer to print an extra hundred jackets or so.

1/16 Of An Inch, 1/32 Of An Inch, And More Damn Math

Many page layout programs have tick marks that measure every 1/16 of an inch or 1/32 of an inch. 1/32 of an inch is 0.03125 inches. So, if your spine bulk is 0.44 inches, we see that we can divide 0.03125 into 0.44 to get 14.08 which is about 14. This means that your spine of 0.44 inches should be measured as fourteen 1/32 inch tick marks.

If your spine width is 0.29, dividing 0.03125 into 0.29, we see that the book is 9.28 1/32 tick marks in width. Because the remainder on division is 0.28, which is about a third, we could measure the spine width as nine full tick marks and about one-third of another tick mark.

When you design your cover, set up the page as the full size of your cover as if it were laid out flat—back, spine, and front. That's how it will be printed. Suppose you have a softcover 6 by 9 book with a spine width of one inch. Your cover layout would be one piece, measuring 13 inches by 9 inches. To mark the start and end of the spine, page layout programs allow you to place rule lines on your page.

So, for example, in Pagemaker, go over to the ruler on the left side of the program, click down and drag and you'll see a blue line, running vertically, following your mouse pointer. Drag that line and place it six inches from the left side of the page. That non-printing, blue rule line shows where the back cover becomes the spine. That will be where the cover folds.

Then, if you drag another rule line and place it the spine-width distance away from the first rule line, you'll see the spine of your book sandwiched between the two rule lines. You can reposition the zero of the scale in Pagemaker by dragging the upper corner of the scale to any point on your document. If you zoom in and carefully drag the scale so that the horizontal scale starts at the first blue rule line, it will be easier to measure and accurately place the second rule line. Then, you can just count the number of tick marks you need for the spine width. In our example, it's easy—we just move one-inch over, because the book's thickness was assumed to be one inch.

Having rule lines telling you where your cover spine starts and ends on your page is very important to design. It's also important to know that your design should allow for the printer's tolerance.

Many POD printers, for example, have a tolerance of 1/16 of an inch. Suppose that you design a cover with a white front, a white back, and a blue spine. This probably wouldn't be the best design, because part of that blue could wrap around onto either the front or back cover. And, worse, part of the white could wrap around to the spine.

When you design a cover always give yourself a margin of safety to allow for printing tolerances. Ask what would happen if the printer was off just a bit. Would the cover still look great? Or would it look like there was a problem? Good design protects against the natural tolerance errors in final placement of the cover.

PMS Colors And Cover Design

Now that we've broached the topic of cover color, we'll address it in more detail. First, many, but not all, POD printers run book covers through a full four-color printing process, so you can use as many colors on the cover as you want and the cost will be the same. This is because along with your cover, many other covers are printed.

With conventional offset printing, for each new color you want on the cover, the cover must be run through the press again.

Fortunately, all colors can be composed of only *three* primary colors plus black. This means full color only requires four passes of the paper through the press. This is why full color is sometimes called "four color." However, if you use less than full color, you save a bit of money in printing costs. And, many quality covers are designed using only one or two PMS colors.

PMS stands for Pantone™ Matching System. You can learn more about this at the website pantone.com.

Imagine that you want to use a very particular shade of purple. Rather than passing the cover paper through the printer three times, once for each primary color, to create the correct blend of purple, you could imagine creating the properly-colored ink and pouring it into the printer.

Then, you print in that one color, and out comes the exact blend of purple you wanted. One pass through the printer. Not three. That saves money. But, how do you know that the color the printer is using exactly matches the color you specify?

The answer is PMS. PMS are "standard" colors and a system of matching colors. There are thousands upon thousands of PMS colors from which to choose. For example, in addition to standard printing black, you could have a darker, richer black, or a muddy black, or countless preestablished variations.

Suppose the color you want happens to be Pantone 527C (which, incidentally, is composed of 12-1/2 parts of Pantone Purple and 3-1/2 parts of Pantone Green). You just tell your printer that you want Pantone 527C and out comes the purple you wanted.

To see how the colors look on paper, you can purchase Pantone color formula guides or swatches, which are printed strips of paper pinned together consisting of all the Pantone colors. You can leaf through the strips and find the colors you like. Or, you can forsake the color strips and rely upon the color's appearance on your computer monitor.

You must be very careful when comparing colors as they appear on a computer monitor because your monitor might display colors differently depending upon your monitor settings. Again, if you're happy with just "purple," that's not a problem. But, if you have your heart set on Pantone 527C, based upon how it looks on your monitor, you want to be sure that your monitor displays Pantone 527C just as the color strips do!

Pantone sells color calibration software to calibrate a computer monitor to the color strips. However, I've seen color calibration software screw up more than one computer system. Hopefully, it's improved by now! To use color calibration software, just follow the software instructions, adjusting monitor settings, such as brightness, until your monitor displays Pantone colors just as they should really look. Then, you can design away and know the colors as they appear on your computer screen should match the final colors on the printed book. Always have the printer provide a color proof of your book, just to be sure.

Pantone suggests buying a new color swatch or color formula guide every few years because the colors might fade. I think that's excessive. Just store your color swatch carefully, and it should last many, many years.

One way to acquire the look of a second color without using a second color is to use a shade (or tint) of the color. Rather than using 100% strength, maybe, you only use a 20% tint. That way you achieve the illusion of multiple colors with only one pass through the printer. That saves some money.

If you have Pagemaker handy, draw a colored box. Then, select "tint" (from Window...Show Colors), set it to less than 100%, draw another box, and you'll see the effect. Incidentally, as long as you have Pagemaker open, notice the little page icon at the bottom of the color palette next to the trash can (Window...Show Colors brings up the palette). If you click on that page icon, it will bring up new color options. If you go to "library" and examine the options in the drop down box, you'll see that you can add new Pantone colors to your document. Depending upon your book printer's requirements, be sure to use either spot colors or process color, i.e., four color, for your cover colors.

Tints of colors are often used for creating lines, filling in text, or creating background color in boxes for text.

Color And Meaning

As you see, color is complex. First, you must decide how much color you need on your cover and balance that against the printing cost. Do you want full color for a picture? Or, are one or two colors enough? Then, you must match the colors as you see them on your computer monitor to the colors as they will actually print or rely upon color swatches. Even the size of a section of color on a page and the colors around it influence how the eye sees the color. But, the real complication of color is how it affects meaning.

Different colors symbolize different things and bring out different emotions in people. For example, it's well known that jail cells in certain colors are more likely to pacify inmates, while other colors tend to enrage inmates and make them more angry and hostile.

Colors have meaning. Some colors are fun. Some are serious. I refer you to pantone.com for more information. Black, for example, is a color of power and strength. Gold is a color of insight and wisdom. But, we must be careful, people often associate yellow with treachery, and yellow is close to gold.

Context of a color's use is important in helping to set meaning. One advantage to hiring a skilled cover designer is that the designer will be aware of the meanings of colors and the psychological implications. You want to design a cover that helps to sell your book. You want your colors to encourage people to buy your books.

In addition to color in cover design, color in logos is very important. I don't claim to be an artist or an expert on color design. But, as the owner of a small publishing company, even if you outsource cover design or hire employees who design covers, you'll want to have a basic understanding of color. It will help you communicate with cover designers and help you understand the marketability and financial costs associated with color choice.

Photo Scanning

One of the easiest ways to get a great cover is to use a great photograph. Creating art is much more difficult than using a relevant picture! It's important to assure that the scanned photo matches the book printer's requirements.

For example, many book printers want photos scanned at 300 dpi. If you don't have a scanner, many book printers are happy to scan your photos for you. Plus, they often can do necessary touch-up work and cropping to improve the photograph.

ISBN Numbers

ISBN numbers can be obtained from R.R. Bowker. (bowker.com). ISBN stands for International Standard Book Number. When you get ISBN numbers, you'll receive a sheet (also called a log book) listing ISBN numbers that are assigned to your company. Typically, a new publisher will be given ten numbers.

You need a new number for each book you publish, so you'll be set to publish ten books. If you produce both a hardcover edition and a softcover edition, each needs a different ISBN. How else would a buyer distinguish the softcover from the hardcover using only the ISBN?

The ISBN is a ten-digit number that uniquely identifies your book and its format (e.g., hardcover, softcover, edition). After you get your ISBN numbers, you're set to get a bar code.

Bar Codes

It's important for all books to have a bar code. Most retailers won't sell books that don't have bar codes, because computers are used to scan products. After acquiring your ISBN number, you can get a bar code.

If you examine the back of any book, you'll see the bar code. The type of bar code you need is referred to as a Bookland EAN Bar Code. Above the actual bar code, you'll see the ten-digit ISBN number. The bar code encodes this information into a computer readable format. In addition, right after the main bar code, you'll see another little bar code that comes attached to it. This part includes price information for the book.

When ordering your barcode, specify the ISBN number and the price. I recommend Bar Code Graphics (Bar Code Graphics, 875 N. Michigan Ave. #2640, Chicago, IL 60611. www.barcode-us.com) which charges $12 to provide a bar code in graphic format.

While you can have a bar code supplied in many formats, the most useful to a publisher is usually the EPS symbol. EPS stands for Encapsulated Postscript, which is a graphics format. You can place your bar code into a Pagemaker document, just as you would any other graphic.

For most newer publishers starting today, all prepress can be done on your computer, either a Mac or a PC. "Camera Ready Copy" is dead or at least dying. Similarly, if you start reading about "paste up" or anything involving glue and sharp blades in a self-publishing book, that's a good indication the book's badly outdated! Everything can be done on your computer. Surprisingly, nearly half of all books printed today are probably still done as camera ready copy.

There are multiple size bar codes available (1.75" by 1" is common). Be sure to allow a white box of text around the bar code so that it can be machine scanned. Also, resizing bar codes is a bad idea. Don't leave too much white space around your bar code or it will look amateurish.

When you print your cover on your laser printer with a postscript print driver, you'll often get the message that the "bar code font is unavailable, print anyway?" Go ahead and print, anyway. The bar code will print adequately. This was a great mystery to me until Gordon Woolf, author of *Publication Production Using PageMaker* (www.worsleypress.com) explained it to me. This error message happens because it's possible to embed fonts into an EPS graphic as well as link to them and Pagemaker keeps track of any font ever used in a file, even if all references to the font are deleted and the font is no longer in use.

There are software programs available that create bar codes. If you produce many books, this can save you some money in the long run. However, you need to be certain that the software renders the bar code adequately. Because of this, I'd recommend a new publisher purchase bar code graphics as needed in graphic file format.

Record Keeping In Publishing

Businesses must keep adequate records. Records are not only necessary for tax reporting, but are necessary for knowing how well you're doing and keeping track of what must be done. Sometimes, you need to know what you've done, so you don't do it again!

Most things that must be recorded will have a 'source' document. For example, for an order from a bookstore, you'd have the purchase order they sent. Some 'source' documents are created on the computer and do not originate on paper. Or, you create them on paper. For example, if Borders Books calls and orders a book, even if you don't have an audio record of the order, you have your notes about the order, including the purchase order number and contact information for Borders.

As a general rule, you should save your source documents. File them away somewhere. Find a system that works for you. For example, you could have individual folders for each distributor and major bookstore with which you deal and another one for miscellaneous orders. Then, depending upon your sales volume, one folder might last for a month or a year. Start a new file for that customer at regular intervals, say monthly. If you have a source document on computer, you might want to print out a copy to include in your paper files.

All computer records should be backed up. For example, if you have online orders or if you receive e-mails notifying you of orders, you should backup that information. Most e-mail is easily backed up. Read your e-mail program's documentation. For example, with MS Outlook Express, if you go to "Tools...Options.. .Maintenance... Store Folder," you'll see the folder that contains your incoming e-mail. Backup that information. Failure to backup important e-mails is a common oversight. For a small publisher, a quick way to regularly backup computer files is to use the commonly available CD-RWs.

After you receive a source document, you'll transfer that information to ledgers. Ledgers are organized ways of collecting related information. They summarize the important information from the source documents. Once information from source documents is transferred to a ledger, you should not need to examine the source documents again. Ledgers can be either paper or on a computer.

Sales Ledger

Sales are the lifeblood of your business. For each sale, you want to record the date of the order, the purchaser, the purchaser's contact information, the address to which the order is to be shipped, the billing address, the purchase order number, the date of the purchase order, and the details of the order. The details of the order include the books ordered and the quantity of each ordered:

Quantity	Book	ISBN	Price	Extended Price

In addition to the information you receive from the company ordering your book, add your own unique order number or order ID which allows you to uniquely identify the order.

Although not formally part of the initial sale, you might want to track if each individual line of the order was shipped and the date shipped or whether the item was backordered. You might also want to track whether or not an invoice has been sent and whether or not the bill has been paid for the order. In addition, you might want to track whether sales tax is due on the order.

Depending upon the sophistication of your record-keeping system, some of this information could be entered automatically by your computer's database. For example, whether sales tax is due could be recorded automatically, based upon the city and state of the order. The unique order number could be assigned by your computer.

If your main ledger is on ledger paper, available at most office supply stores, then, you must manually enter any information you want to track. Many small publishers find good-old-fashioned paper ledgers work quite well. You should transfer your ledger information to a computer database or accounting program. Computers allow easy evaluation and summary of your information.

Payments (Cash Received) Ledger

You must also keep track of all payments your company receives. Record the date of the payment, the source of the payment, the amount of the payment, the purchase order to which the payment corresponds, and your unique order ID. You might also want to record the check number and any other information you find useful.

Expenses Incurred And Expenses Paid

All expenses incurred and expenses paid should be recorded. And, all receipts should be saved. Because legitimate business expenses are tax deductible for your business, it's important to document legitimate business expenses. For example, if you write a check for $500 for office supplies for your business, you want to have the receipt showing what was purchased. This way if you're ever audited by the IRS, you can show that the expense was a legitimate business expense.

In addition to travel and entertainment expenditures, one thing that draws a tax auditor's attention are huge "miscellaneous" expenses. The more detailed your expenses reported on your tax return, the less likely you are to be audited.

Because many of your business purchases will be made with your business checking account, many small publishers use their business checkbook as a proxy for tracking expenses incurred and paid. For example, if you order a bar code for $12, you write a check for $12. That shows you've incurred and paid for a $12 expense.

Some expenses paid for with a check aren't fully tax deductible when the check is written. For example, if you write a check to your printer for $6,000 for 2,000 books, you do not record $6,000 as an immediate expense. As discussed elsewhere, you would record a decrease in cash of $6,000, but you'd record an increase of $6,000 in another asset—inventory. That inventory would sell and the expense would be recorded as it sells as cost-of-goods-sold.

Debits And Credits

As your business grows, you might want to invest the time to take a double-entry accounting class at your local community college. Double-entry accounting is very robust and designed to record all financial changes in your business. To help you learn double-entry accounting, I recommend *Keeping The Books: Basic Record-Keeping and Accounting For The Small Business* by Linda Pinson and Jerry Jinnett. I also recommend *The McGraw-Hill 36-Hour Accounting Course* by Robert Dixon and Harold Arnett. I review both books on entrepreneurbooks.com.

The underlying principle of double-entry accounting is that for every accounting transaction, two accounts are affected. One entry made to the accounts is referred to as a debit. The other entry is referred to as a credit. The total value of credits must equal the total value of debits. Debits are always listed on the left hand side of the account and credits are listed on the right hand side:

Account Name

Debit	Credit

For example, when you paid $6,000 for printed books, you'd credit cash $6,000 and you'd debit the title's inventory $6,000. Credits decrease asset accounts, while debits increase asset accounts.

Inventory and cash are both asset accounts. Thus, cash was decreased by $6,000, and inventory was increased by $6,000. In addition to asset accounts, there are liability accounts, revenue accounts, and expense accounts.

Crediting Sales

When one book is sold at $19.95, two different accounting transactions occur. First, the sale is recorded. Sales are credited $19.95. Then, if money is received for the sale, be it cash or check, 'Cash' is debited $19.95. Debits increase 'Cash,' because 'Cash' is an asset account. I always think of the 'creditor' as giving to the 'debtor.' Sales give to cash. If cash isn't received, then, 'Accounts Receivable' for that vendor is debited $19.95. Money owed to us, or accounts receivable, is another asset account.

In addition to making the sale and receiving payment or the promise to pay, inventory and cost-of-goods-sold (cogs) expense are also affected by selling one copy. The per-unit cost of our books is $3. So, our asset account 'Inventory' is credited by $3, which represents a decrease in inventory. Then, cogs expense, an expense account, is increased by $3 with a debit.

Accounting Programs And Publishing Databases

As you become more familiar with double-entry accounting, a good off-the-shelf accounting software program is MYOB (Mind Your Own Business). For people who tend to prefer the simpler single-entry accounting, Quicken Quickbooks is recommended. Many self-publishers use Quickbooks, MYOB, or another basic accounting program.

Special software database programs exist which are designed to deal with the business of book publishing. Pub123 (www.adams-blake.com), which is based upon MS Access, is one such program. Publishers' Assistant (www.upperaccess.com), Acumen (www.acumenbook.com), Myrlyn (www.myrlyn.com), and The Cat's Pajamas (www.tcpj.com) are other database programs for publishers.

MS Access also has an 'order entry' database that can be modified to serve a small publishing company.

The advantage to specialty databases is that they can easily deal with author royalties, book returns, and other aspects unique to the book publishing industry. However, when you're just starting, you might only publish your own books, so you probably can get by with a standard accounting program.

Sources Of Other Income

As a small business owner, in addition to tracking your business income and sales, you should also record *all other sources of income unrelated to your business*. For example, if you receive a $50 mail-in rebate for a personal computer purchase, you should record the source of the payment.

Even though this purchase is unrelated to your business, you want to track all sources of income. Keep source documents. You might also want to track your personal expenses in a program such as Quicken. Many individuals gain significant insight into their spending habits by tracking their expenses with Quicken.

The reason to record all sources of personal income is to document them in the event that you are audited by the IRS. It's crucial for small business owners to document *sources of income* as well as expenses. For example, if your brother-in-law repays a $4,000 loan to you and you deposit the money in your personal bank account, you don't want the IRS to mistakenly believe those are book sales that you haven't reported as income! Document all sources of nonbusiness income!

Review Copies Given Away

Record all review copies given away. Record who receives the review copy and his or her contact information. If you send a review copy, be sure to follow up to see if the reviewer received your book. Ask the reviewer if he or she will be reviewing your book. Such follow-up is very effective.

The Power Of Accounting

The advantage to using a full accounting program and double-entry accounting is that it will give you insight into your company. This will help you record your expenses and liabilities as they occur. The checkbook is only a very rough proxy to how well you're doing for most self-publishers.

For example, you might owe money that isn't recorded in your checkbook. Maybe you charged a bar code to your credit card, for example. When you're starting, you might just wait until you receive the credit card bill, pay it by company check, and record it into your checkbook. That's the first posting of this expense to your business records.

While this sometimes works if you have a *small* level of business activity, as you grow, you won't be able to mentally track money you owe next month and in the following months. You'll need to do more than just 'remember' that you have a $12 expense coming due next month and be sure that amount is in the checkbook!

Imagine having three or four books being reprinted this month. Each one will represent several thousand dollars you'll need to pay next month. Plus, you're publishing a new book. That's several thousand more dollars you must pay. You have two covers being designed and will owe the designer a couple thousand dollars. You purchased some office supplies with your credit card and that bill will also come due next month. That's too much to 'remember.'

Unless you're tracking the money you'll owe and when you'll need to pay it, you run the risk of having bills coming due and not having the money to pay them. This is called a "cash flow crunch." *Many businesses which could have become very successful failed because of poor record-keeping and financial planning.* And, all it would have taken *not* to fail is a bit of learning, a bit of time spent in keeping good records, and a bit of time spent looking at what your accounting data is telling you!

The Holy Grail Of Publishing

The Power Of Trademarks, Copyrights, And A Profitable Series

When you finished writing your book, you probably went to the U.S. Copyright Office online (www.loc.gov/copyright), downloaded the proper forms (Form TX or the Short Form TX for books), filled them in, mailed the forms with a copy of your book and the copyright fee to The Library of Congress. That's all there is to getting a copyright. It's easy and it's the first thing you should do when you've finished writing a book.

Copyrighting a book represents protecting your intellectual property. I discuss intellectual property in more detail in *Thinking Like An Entrepreneur*. Intellectual property is sometimes called intellectual capital. 'Property' and 'capital' imply that books have a financial worth.

Unfortunately, just because we've written and copyrighted a book doesn't mean the book has any value. If the book doesn't sell, it has little value. But, sometimes a book will take off and become popular. If that happens with a book you've authored, you'll do well. If you couldn't protect your intellectual capital, other people could print your book and undercut your price. But, with a copyright of your book, you can legally prevent people from exploiting your book. You will be the one who controls how the book is exploited for profit.

Valuation Of A Copyright

Here is the correct theoretical way to value a copyright. Calculations like this are always tenuous as the past isn't always the best guide to the future!

Your goal is to estimate the future cash flows from ownership of such rights (copyright or trademark) and, then, using the time value of money, discount all estimated future cash flows to the present. You should allow for any likely future events that will change the value of the revenue stream to you. In particular, give less weight to years farther in the future as more can go wrong to devalue such a right over a longer period of time. This adjustment is *in addition* to the fact that years farther into the future are discounted more due to the time value of money. Years farther into the future also represent less certainty.

This calculated present value represents the value of this intellectual "asset." Then, if you're a buyer, you try to buy the asset for much less, giving your purchase a margin of safety. If you're a seller, try to sell the asset for much more, giving yourself a financial windfall!

Before doing such a calculation, first ask *what would be the cost to replicate a similar stream of future profits by creating an equivalent property*. Examine how stable you feel the future sales/profits will be for the property and how much marketing effort must go into *maintaining* the title's stream of profitability.

For example, if a book doesn't have a track record, or anything making it especially unique (e.g., a famous author) relative to a new *similar* book by another *similar* author, then this method of copyright valuation *shouldn't* be used. *You'd do just as well launching your own book on the topic as you'd do buying the rights to something unestablished.*

It's nearly impossible to predict the success of a new book. In other words, it's dangerous to say, "Gosh, this is a great book. I know it will do well" and use the future revenue calculation method to value it. It's a different story if you're dealing with a constantly bestselling author's new book whose sales might be more easily predicted. A problem with such calculations is it's easy to mislead yourself into believing what you want! Doing these calculations objectively is much more difficult.

A book with a sales history allows a calculation of the future revenue stream the book is expected to yield. Expected does not mean guaranteed! The current value of this future revenue stream can be calculated by discounting all the estimated future cash flows back to the present.

When you account for the time value of money, you'll need to choose a discount rate. Here is where most people do something silly. They *change* the discount rate to account for the rate of return they demand or to compensate for the risk of the property they are valuing. This is fundamentally poor advice. Small changes in the discount rate too greatly affect valuation and there is no proper way to match up real risk with discount rate. Rather, fix the discount rate at one value for all similar properties and evaluate risk factors *qualitatively*. This allows you to make value comparisons between different, but similar, properties.

Annuity Valuation

Let's work the simplest case. Assume a particular title sells 5,000 copies every year. Also assume that it earns the publisher $3 per copy sold. We'll assume that the title keeps selling at the same rate and that any inflationary costs in book production are offset by increases in the retail price of the book.

This book can be treated as an annuity paying $15,000 per year. The formula to value an annuity is: $V = CF/D$ where CF is the annual net cash flow provided by the annuity and D is the appropriate discount rate, which corresponds to the "fair" rate of return from investing in the annuity. Estimating an appropriate D for books isn't trivial. We'll use 15%.

$$V = \$15,000/0.15 = \$100,000$$

This title has a calculated value of $100,000. If we used 10% as the discount rate, the title's value is $150,000. If we used 20% as the discount rate, the title's value is $75,000. From a buyer's perspective, the real danger is that book sales will fall off drastically after a few years.

The formula to value a series of cash flow payments for n years is:

$$V = CF_1/(1+D) + CF_2/(1+D)^2 + CF_3/(1+D)^3 + ... + CF_n/(1+D)^n$$

where CF_i is the cash flow in year i and D is again the discount rate. $(1+D)^2$ means take $(1+D)$ times $(1+D)$. $(1+D)^3$ means take $(1+D)$ times $(1+D)$ times $(1+D)$, etc. $(1+D)^n$ means take $(1+D)$ times itself n times. You'll want a calculator to do these calculations.

Let's assume the title earns $15,000 per year for each of the next five years, and the book goes out-of-print after that (CF_i is $15,000 for years 1 to 5).

$$V = \$15,000 \ (1/(1.15) + 1/(1.15)^2 + 1/(1.15)^3 + 1/(1.15)^4 + 1/(1.15)^5)$$
$$= \$15,000 \ (0.870 + .756 + .658 + .572 + .497) = \$50,295$$

Under these assumptions, the book's value is $50,295. Notice that the present value of the book is less than just five times $15,000. This is due to the time value of money.

If you're an investor in the stock market, you might recognize the above annuity valuation formulas as special cases of dividend discount calculations. All financial assets are theoretically valued the same way. Estimate the stream of future profits the investment yields. Discount that cash flow stream to the present. The result is the present value of the investment or asset.

If you want to learn more about stock valuation, I recommend my own book, *Becoming An Investor: Building Wealth By Investing In Stocks, Bonds, And Mutual Funds*.

I wanted to give you the above short discussion of the proper way to value an intellectual asset as the present value of the future revenue stream that the asset generates for you. However, unless you're actively buying and selling the rights to books, you probably don't need to worry about learning this. There are many successful publishers who don't understand the proper valuation of intellectual assets, but who earn hundreds of thousands or even millions of dollars a year in the book trade! Even if you can't value the darn thing, you can still create it, sell it, and put the checks in the bank as they roll in!

However, as you grow your publishing company, if you buy, sell, or negotiate the rights to books, being able to estimate the value of a copyright might prove useful.

Ball Park Estimates Of Advances And Revenue Streams

Small publishers should be careful not to pay an author too large an advance. And, estimating the future profits from your own titles doesn't need to involve the formalism previously discussed.

Using very basic math, we could ask the following: Assume that Bill Clinton is paid a $10 million advance for his new book. How many copies must the publisher sell to recover the advance?

Assume the book has a retail price of $20. Also assume the author is paid a 10% royalty ($2 per book. Often hardcover royalties are 12% or 15%, but never mind that). Assume the publisher expects to earn $1.50 per book after all expenses, including the payment of royalties.

It might seem that we should divide the $10 million advance by the $2 royalty and conclude that the publisher must sell 5 million copies to break even. That isn't quite true. If the publisher sells 5 million copies, the expense of author royalties is $10 million. That's true. But, we've assumed the publisher is able to earn $1.50 a copy for each book sold if a royalty of $2 is already subtracted from that copy. Thus, if the publisher sells 5 million copies, the publisher *earns* $7.5 million profit.

If we add the royalty per book to our estimated profit per book for a total of $3.50 and we divide that into $10 million, we get the true break-even level of sales of 2.86 million copies.

Working backwards, let's assume we've sold 2.86 million copies. The *earned* amount of the advance is $2 per copy times 2.86 million copies or $5.72 million. If we hadn't paid an advance at all, but only royalties as they were earned, by our estimates, we'd have earned $1.50 per copy times 2.86 million copies or $4.29 million. That $4.29 million would represent our share of the profits if there hadn't been an advance, but if royalties were paid as the book sold. However, there was an advance of $10 million. Of that, $5.72 million was earned, leaving us with a 'loss' of about $4.28 million on the advance that was just covered by the amount we 'earned' on the first 2.86 million sales, i.e., we break even. (The small difference between $4.28 million and $4.29 million represents round off error—break even was actually 2,857,142 copies)

Advances aren't determined only by what the publisher needs to break even. Giving a $10 million advance would be pointless if only 2.86 million books sold. The publisher wouldn't earn anything!

Maximum advances should be determined by a conservative estimate of how many copies the publisher anticipates selling in a relatively short time period. If we simply divide the advance by the royalty per book, we see how many copies the publisher expects to sell. Five million copies or more in Bill's case.

While celebrity advances are often determined by competitive bidding by multiple large publishers, as small publishers, we can't get into bidding wars with other publishers. Publishers increase advances to get desirable authors. "Desirable" is determined by author marketability.

There are far more manuscripts than publishers and submitted manuscripts are already written, so the advance isn't used to sustain the author as he writes his opus. It seems the only purpose of the advance is to make the writer happy.

To see what other publishers claim they pay as advances, examine *Writer's Market* and assume the lower end of their stated range is actually paid. You'll see many publishers offer no advance or a very minimal advance of a few hundred dollars.

Back to Bill's book. We see we need to sell about three million copies to break even. Most bestsellers have two or three years of great sales. Then sales plateau. Thus, we see we need to be able to sell about a million books a year for the first three years to break even in the first three years. Most of those sales will probably occur early, and any sales into future years will earn profits. Thus, the question for the publisher is: Do we believe we can sell three million copies of this book? Any less, and the publisher loses money.

When setting advances, look at two different numbers to help you decide what's appropriate: 1) The total book sales you anticipate; 2) the number of sales you need to break-even to cover a given advance. Also examine what other, similar publishers pay.

Some publishers pay an advance equal to one-half the royalties earned if the first press run were to sell out. So, if you're paying a per-book royalty of $2 and the first press run is 5,000 copies, the advance would be $5,000.

Self-Publisher Break Even

Sometimes new publishers get confused by another variation of this theme. Suppose you can earn $4 profit per book for your self-published book. Assume that the book costs $3 per unit to produce.

You produce 3,000 copies for $9,000. How many copies must you sell to breakeven?

Answer: Add profit back to the per unit cost for a total of $7 per unit. Then, divide that into $9,000 to get 1,286. That's how many units you must sell to break even. This is because with each unit sold, you not only earn $4 per unit, but you also recover $3 per unit that was invested in the inventory.

Backlist—Revenue Stream Per Book

After a few years, book sales often plateau. The plateau is a very interesting place to be in book sales. Many books sell several thousand copies each year. If you have a book that consistently sells 3,000 copies a year and it earns about $4 per book, the book generates a revenue stream of about $12,000 per year.

Clearly a self-publisher couldn't get by on $12,000 per year. But, what happens if the publisher has five or ten books in print, each of which earns similar profits? This is the power of having a strong backlist. In publishing, "front list" is used to refer to the books you're currently bringing out. "Back list" are those books which you've published in the past and which continue to sell. If asked to identify a "holy grail" to successful book publishing, many small publishers would identify having a strong backlist. View each of your titles as an investment for the future.

Remainder The Duds

Not every book will do well. Almost every publisher has at least one title that is downright embarrassing! Remainder dealers buy books on the cheap. You can remainder any books that are doing really poorly. Why sit on useless inventory, when you can get a tax write-off by remaindering it?

For example, if you have $10,000 in inventory and are only selling two books a year and you remainder your books for $2,000, you report a loss of $8,000. If you pay 44% in federal and state taxes, you instantly save $3,520 in taxes because this loss offsets other income. If you recover $7 per book for those two crummy books sold each year, it would take you about 250 years to recoup that tax savings via actual book sales!

You can choose the tax year during which you decide to remainder your books. If you anticipate being in a higher tax bracket next year, you might wait and remainder the books next year. But, if you're facing a large tax liability this year, you could remainder them in the current year. In either case, I hope you won't have to remainder too many books!

There's also a psychological advantage to cutting projects that aren't working and just taking space. Cutting these projects frees you to concentrate upon something else, such as a new book that might do better!

Have A Bestseller

If your small publishing company has a bestselling book, you'll do well financially. Today, it's common for bestselling books to sell several hundred thousand to a million copies or more. While all publishers hope for a bestseller, it's difficult to know which books will evolve into bestsellers. Many small publishers do quite well and they never have a bestseller. Their profits come from a strong backlist.

However, the big publishing houses take a "shot on goal" approach to selling books. They're looking for bestsellers. And, they're willing to publish ten or twenty books to find one bestseller. Those books that don't show some bestseller potential might be added to their backlist or dumped.

Each book from a big publishing house is usually viewed as a speculation. It's a test. If the book seems to have bestseller status, the publishing house will promote it aggressively. But, if there's a good indication the book will only be a modest seller, it won't be promoted heavily. The resources will be thrown into promoting a title with more potential.

Self-publishers nearly always aggressively work to promote their titles. A huge part of the effort behind a self-published book is the time spent writing the manuscript. Very few self-publishers would spend six months writing a book and then decide to dump it!

A big advantage to publishing other authors is that you don't invest time in book authorship. Given the time investment to write a book and the fact that an author can be a valuable salesperson for his or her book and add marketing capability, author royalties are really a profitable expense!

It's interesting to note that author royalties are usually based upon the number of books *sold* (per copy sold royalty) and not on the *profits* earned by the publisher. This creates an inherent conflict between what's in the best interests of the author and of the publisher. For example, it would be to an author's advantage for the publisher to heavily promote his or her book, even if the publisher doesn't recover the promotional cost.

Imagine, for example, taking out full page newspaper ads throughout the country for a book. That would generate sales. And, the author would collect great royalties. But, it probably wouldn't generate *sufficient* sales for the publisher to *recover* his investment in placing the ads. Further, that exposure helps to create name-brand recognition for the author.

An important question is: "Who benefits from name-brand recognition created by publicity?"

Contracts play an important role in book publishing. Who owns the rights to the book? Further, what are the contractual obligations of the author to the publisher and the publisher to the author?

As we noted before, bestselling books beget bestselling books. I could name dozens of authors who had a great first book which made the bestseller lists. Then, they did a follow up book that was only so-so. It also made the bestseller lists. Then, often, they write a third so-so book, and it too makes the bestseller lists! Those second and third books wouldn't have become bestsellers if it hadn't been for the first book!

Many book publishers insist upon acquiring the rights to an author's next title. If the publisher spends a lot of money to promote an author and the author becomes a bestselling author, the publisher wants to be assured of participating in the author's future success. So, that future participation is written into the first book's contract.

Trademark And Copyright Conclusion

I want to reemphasize a key point: When a book is promoted, two sources of value are created. First is the present profitability to both the author and the publisher. Second is the enhanced celebrity level of the author which leads to future author marketability which enhances the author's value.

I can't help but recall a line from *The Sound Of Music*. Talent agent Max Detweiler overhears a local choir and says he should scout the area for talent.

Captain Von Trapp observes, "They get the fame, and you get the money."

Max retorts, "It is unfair. But, someday that shall all be changed. I shall get the fame, *too*."

Some savvy publishers have taken that speculation to heart. They want to benefit from enhanced future awareness created by present author publicity. We're not talking about enhanced future profitability of the presently-promoted title. Rather, we're talking about enhancing the salability of *other* titles, such as an author's follow-up work.

What authors and publishers can promote is an *identity*. Identities are usually trademarked (uspto.gov). Consider a booksigning for a title in the *For Dummies*^{TM} series.

"For Dummies^{TM}" is a trademarked expression, and IDG Books has used the same basic cover look and feel for all its "For Dummies^{TM}" titles. It does this to create a recognizable identity. With each book promoted, the identity is promoted, enhancing the value of the trademark to the publisher.

If a title is added to the popular trademarked series, the title becomes easier to promote than a title standing alone. And, just as a copyright can have financial value, trademarks can also obtain considerable value if you ever decide to sell your publishing company or sell the rights to an imprint of your publishing house. In this way, publishers can get the fame, too!

Self-Publishing As A Business

I hope this book hasn't left you disillusioned with self-publishing and independent publishing. Publishing is a business, and there's a lot to know. But, don't be afraid of making mistakes. You can learn as you go. That's what most publishers do. And, many of them now sell more than 100,000 books each year. Don't be afraid to ask questions. That's how we learn. Be sure to network with other publishers.

What drives profitability in the publishing business? Selling more books is the key, but how do you sell more books? Each successful publisher seems to find sales outlets and a promotional strategy that suits the publisher. Two significant factors affecting sales are the book's topic and the author's skills in promoting it. Give those consideration with each title you produce.

While I've discussed the dangers and risks associated with publishing (for example, the danger of overprinting a first press run), I want to emphasize that *self-publishing is a relatively low-risk business*. Many self-publishers start with little money and risk very little money.

But, on the upside, self-publishing offers great potential reward. Some self-published books will turn into bestsellers. Others will turn into strong backlist titles, which generate consistent annual profits. Some of your titles might interest larger publishers.

Your company can acquire substantial market value through a strong trademarked imprint, one bestselling title, or a solid backlist.

I wish you the best of success and happiness in starting and running your own book publishing company! Peter

Select Resources For Small Publishers

Books:

The Prepublishing Handbook: What You Should Know Before You Publish Your First Book by Patricia J. Bell

The Complete Guide to Self-Publishing: Everything You Need to Know to Write, Publish, Promote, and Sell Your Own Book by Tom Ross and Marilyn Ross

Make Money Self-Publishing: Learn How From Fourteen Successful Small Publishers by Suzanne P. Thomas

The Self-Publishing Manual: How to Write, Print and Sell Your Own Book by Dan Poynter

Publishing For Profit: Successful Bottom-Line Management For Book Publishers by Thomas Woll

Book Publishing: A Basic Introduction by John Dessauer

Marketing and Promoting Your Own Seminars and Workshops by Fred Gleeck

How To Publish and Promote Online by M. J. Rose and Angela Adair-Hoy

1001 Ways to Market Your Books by John Kremer

Jump Start Your Book Sales: A Money-Making Guide for Authors, Independent Publishers and Small Presses by Tom and Marilyn Ross

Book Design and Production For The Small Publisher by Malcolm E. Barker.

The Non-Designers Design Book by Robin Williams

Type and Layout by Colin Wheildon

Publication Production Using PageMaker: A Guide To Using Adobe PageMaker 7 For The Production of Newspapers, Newsletters, Magazines And Other Formatted Publications by Gordon Woolf

Trash-Proof News Releases: The Surefire Way to Get Publicity by
    Paul J. Krupin
Media Magic: Profit and Promote with Free Media Promotion
    by Marisa D'Vari
Grassroots Marketing: Getting Noticed in a Noisy World by Shel
    Horowitz
*Keeping The Books: Basic Record-Keeping and Accounting For
    The Small Business* by Linda Pinson and Jerry Jinnett.
*Small Time Operator: How To Start Your Own Small Business,
    Keep Your Books, Pay Your Taxes, And Stay Out Of Trouble!* by
    Bernard B. Kamoroff.

Websites:

http://publishing.about.com
http://hometown.aol.com/catspawpre/ToolShed.html
    (Pat Bell's site)
http://ParaPublishing.com (Dan Poynter's site)
http://www.pma-online.org (Publishers Marketing Association)
http://www.bookmarket.com
http://www.communicationcreativity.com
    (Tom and Marilyn Ross's site)
http://www.bookwire.com
http://www.bookzonepro.com/resources/
http://www.vikingop.com (Viking Office Products often offers free
    shipping on orders of $25 or more—when purchasing mailing
    folders and boxes, shipping costs are a big factor.)
http://www.publish-L.com (e-mail discussion list for small
    publishers. Highly recommend.)
http://www.hslc.org/archives/publish-l.html (Publish-L Archives)
http://www.pub-forum.net
    (Pub Forum, another e-mail discussion list for small publishers.)
http://www.book-clearing-house.com (Book Clearing House, a
    fulfillment/order taking company. They offer an 800 order
    number, if you don't wish to establish your own and you can fill
    the orders yourself, if you want.)

http://www.psscnj.com
  (Publishers Storage And Shipping, Inc. A fulfillment company.)
http://www.GuestFinder.com
  (A directory of authors available for media interviews.)
http://www.NewsBuzz.com
http://www.imediafax.com (For sending fax press releases)
http://www.yudkin.com (Information for authors and publishers)
http://www.tshore.com
  (Thomson-Shore, Inc., a highly-regarded book printer.)
http://www.bookprinters.com
  (McNaughton & Gunn, another highly-regarded book printer)
http://www.lightningsource.com (Ingram's POD Printer)
http://www.replicabooks.com (Baker & Taylor's POD Printer)
http://www.fidlardoubleday.com (Highly-respected POD Printer)
http://www.entrepreneurbooks.com
  (My reviews of small business books)
http://www.thinkinglike.com (My small Business Website)
http://www.ideacafe.com (Small Business Website with a great
  bulletin board system for asking questions.)
http://www.midwestbookreview.com
  (Resources and articles for publishers and information about
  how the review process works. Highly recommended.)
http://www.bowkerlink.com (For adding titles to *Books In Print*)
http://www.barcode-us.com (Bar Code Graphics, Inc.)

Other Resources:

TLC Graphics (Professional Book Design)
Tami Dever
Phone: 512-292-8798
Email: tamara@tlcgraphics.com
http://www.TLCGraphics.com (Information about hiring and
working with a professional book designer.)

Index

Printed in the United States
121487LV00004B/508/A

9 780967 162430